Anti-Inflammatory Cookbook for Beginners

"Discover 250 authentic, simple, healthy, and delicious recipes, ideal for those just starting out, and pair them with a 28-day eating plan. Choose anti-inflammatory foods in the right amounts to reduce oxidative stress and the risk of systemic inflammation."

Author Name:

ANGELA WARD

INDEX

Introduction:

Welcome to the Anti-Inflammatory Kitchen

Hello, and welcome to your new culinary adventure! This book was created with the intention of guiding you through the wonderful world of anti-inflammatory cooking. But before we dive into the delicious recipes and secrets of an anti-inflammatory diet, it is important to understand the motivation behind this journey.

Inflammation is a word we hear often, but what does it really mean? In simple terms, it is our body's response to emergency situations such as an injury or infection. It is our body's way of fighting off threats and beginning the healing process. Acute inflammation is a healthy and necessary response.

But what happens when inflammation becomes chronic? Chronic inflammation is a low-grade process that persists over time, often without obvious symptoms. This persistent inflammation has been connected to a wide range of health problems, including obesity, cardiovascular disease, and autoimmune diseases.

The good news is that we can **influence inflammation** through our food and lifestyle choices. And that is exactly what you will learn in this book.

Before you begin, keep in mind that this book does not promise a miracle cure for any medical condition. Rather, it is an invitation to explore the power of healthy foods and lifestyle habits to promote overall well-being.

In the following pages, you will discover:

The difference between inflammatory and anti-inflammatory foods.

How to plan anti-inflammatory meals and organize your kitchen.

Delicious and nutritious recipes for breakfast, lunch, and dinner.

Tips for managing stress, improving sleep, and maintaining a healthy lifestyle.

Resources for further study.

If you already struggle with your health in any way, it is imperative that you see your physician before making any significant alterations to your diet. Anti-inflammatory cooking is a journey of wellness and discovery, and we are excited to accompany you on this adventure. Are you ready? Lace up your aprons, and let's start cooking together!

What is inflammation?

Inflammation is the body's natural response to damage or irritation, such as infection, injury, or other challenges to tissue integrity. It is a fundamental part of the body's defense system and helps to repair and protect the body from injury and infection. Inflammation is a complex process involving a number of chemical and cellular reactions.

Here is how it works in a simplified way

Inflammation signal: When the body detects damage or a pathogen, the immune system releases chemical signals called cytokines. These signals alert the body to the need for an inflammatory response.

Dilation of blood vessels: Blood vessels in the affected area dilate to increase blood flow. This brings more blood, oxygen, and nutrients to the affected area to promote healing.

Increased vascular permeability: Blood vessels become more permeable, allowing immune system cells, such as white blood cells, to reach the site of inflammation more easily.

Accumulation of white blood cells: White blood cells, or leukocytes, accumulate in the inflamed area to fight infection or remove damaged cellular debris.

Scar tissue production: Once the pathogen has been eliminated or the damage has been repaired, the body begins to produce scar tissue to rebuild damaged tissue.

Resolution: Eventually, the inflammation subsides, and the tissue heals. This stage is essential for restoring balance in the body.

Inflammation is a fundamental process for survival and healing, but it can become problematic if it becomes chronic. Inflammation that persists over time is linked to a number of different diseases and ailments, including coronary heart disease, diabetes, rheumatoid arthritis, and other autoimmune conditions. Consequently, maintaining a healthy balance in inflammation is important for overall health and is one of the basic tenets of anti-inflammatory cooking.

Types of inflammation:

Acute inflammation: This is the most common form of inflammation and is an immediate response of the body to injury or infection. Acute inflammation is usually short-lived and serves to protect the body from further damage. Examples of acute inflammation include the swelling and redness of a burn or the inflammation of a wound.

Chronic inflammation: Chronic inflammation is a long-term form of inflammation that can persist for weeks, months, or even years. This form of inflammation is often less obvious than acute inflammation and may be associated with more serious health conditions. Causes of chronic inflammation can include an unhealthy lifestyle, such as a diet rich in processed foods or excess stress.

Common causes of chronic inflammation:

Unbalanced diet: Chronic inflammation can be exacerbated by consuming an excessive amount of meals that are heavy in refined carbohydrates, saturated fats, and processed foods. On the other hand, eating a diet that is abundant in fruits and vegetables, as well as lean proteins and healthy fats, will help lower inflammation.

Obesity: Obesity is often associated with chronic inflammation, as excess adipose tissue can produce inflammatory cytokines.

Chronic stress: Persistent stress can trigger an inflammatory response in the body.

Tobacco smoking: Smoking is known to be a powerful trigger of chronic inflammation.

Autoimmune diseases: These conditions cause the immune system to mistakenly attack one's own body, leading to chronic inflammation.

Health risks of chronic inflammation:

Cardiovascular disease: Chronic inflammation can damage artery walls, contributing to heart disease.

Type 2 diabetes: Inflammation can interfere with insulin function, contributing to the development of type 2 diabetes.

Arthritis: Joint inflammation is a characteristic feature of arthritis.

Inflammatory bowel disease: Chronic inflammation of the intestines is associated with conditions such as Crohn's disease and ulcerative colitis.

Neurological diseases: Inflammation that persists over time may play a role in the development of neurological conditions such as Parkinson's disease and Alzheimer's disease.

Anti-inflammatory cooking aims to reduce chronic inflammation through a balanced diet and lifestyle. It relies on fresh foods that are rich in antioxidants and natural anti-inflammatory substances. Although it does not promise a cure, it can contribute to overall well-being by reducing the factors that fuel chronic inflammation. Before making major dietary or lifestyle changes, it's crucial to speak with a doctor, especially if you have any health issues already.

Chapter 1:

Fundamentals of Anti-Inflammatory Cooking

Ancient wisdom teaches us that "we are what we eat." This adage resonates with a fundamental truth: Our bodies are complex machines, and the fuel we choose to provide them with has a profound impact on our health. In the modern world, chronic inflammation has become a growing concern. But what does "anti-inflammatory cooking" really mean?

Inflammatory foods vs. anti-inflammatory foods

- ### Foods to avoid

In our quest for comfort and taste satisfaction, we often find ourselves consuming foods that can fuel the fire of inflammation in our bodies. Because they are usually high in refined carbs, saturated fats, and artificial additives, these meals might stimulate the immune system to respond in an inflammatory manner. This can be a cause for concern for those with autoimmune diseases. This category includes a wide variety of foods and beverages, some examples of which are quick-service restaurants, packaged snacks, and sugary drinks.

- ### Beneficial foods

On the other end of the food spectrum, we find a host of foods rich in anti-inflammatory properties. Green leafy vegetables, antioxidant-rich fruits, fatty fish such as salmon, and nuts are all allies in the fight against inflammation. These foods are loaded with nutrients that can not only help put out the fire of inflammation but can also promote healing and overall well-being.

The basics of an anti-inflammatory diet

A balance between fat, protein, and carbohydrates

A well-balanced, anti-inflammatory diet pays attention to the ratio of fat, protein, and carbohydrates. Inflammation can be prevented, and blood sugar levels stabilized by avoiding too much of any of these ingredients. Vegetable oils such as olive oil, lean proteins such as chicken, and whole-grain carbohydrates such as oats are wise choices.

Healthy choices of carbohydrates and fats

Not all carbohydrates and fats are created equal. The anti-inflammatory diet favors complex carbohydrates, such as those found in whole grains and vegetables, which release energy gradually and prevent spikes in blood sugar. Healthy fats, such as those found in avocados and walnuts, include a high concentration of omega-3 fatty acids, which are well known for the anti-inflammatory properties they possess.

Managing sugar and sweeteners

Effects of sugar on inflammation

Sugar, present in many forms in our foods, is often a catalyst for inflammation. Excess blood sugar can trigger a cascade of inflammatory events in our bodies. Reducing the consumption of added sugars is an important step on the road to anti-inflammatory cooking.

Natural alternatives to sweeteners

To satisfy our craving for sweetness without resorting to refined sugar, we can explore more natural alternatives such as honey, maple syrup, and stevia. These sweeteners can provide a touch of sweetness without causing blood sugar spikes.

Taken together, these fundamentals of anti-inflammatory cooking are the foundation for a diet that aims to promote health and keep chronic inflammation under control. On this journey to wellness, remember that mindfulness and balance are key.

Chapter 2:

Menu Planning

Menu planning is a crucial step in adopting an effective anti-inflammatory diet effectively. This is not only about what you eat but also how you organize your diet in a sustainable way.

Planning Anti-Inflammatory Meals for the Week.

A well-planned week is the foundation of a successful anti-inflammatory diet. Here are some practical strategies for planning anti-inflammatory meals:

Prepare a shopping list: Before going to the supermarket, write down a list of ingredients needed for planned recipes. This will reduce the temptation to buy unhealthy foods.

Meal Variation: Be sure to include a variety of anti-inflammatory foods in your weekly diet. This not only keeps the eating plan interesting but also provides a wide range of nutrients.

Batch cooking: Preparing large quantities of food at a time can simplify meal preparation during the week. Dishes can be stored in smaller portions for use when needed.

Kitchen Preparation

A well-organized kitchen is essential to facilitate the preparation of anti-inflammatory meals. Here are some guidelines:

Purchase essential tools: Invest in tools such as high-quality nonstick pans, wooden or plastic cutting boards, and sharp knives to simplify meal preparation.

Organize space: Keep countertops and cabinets neat. Anti-inflammatory ingredients such as spices, oils, and whole grains should be easily accessible.

Regular cleaning: Keeping the kitchen clean and hygienic is essential for safe meal preparation. Clean after each use to avoid cross-contamination.

In summary, menu planning and kitchen organization are two pillars of anti-inflammatory cooking. Good planning simplifies meal preparation and reduces temptations to opt for less healthy foods. A well-organized kitchen makes it easier to create nutritious and delicious meals.

Chapter 3:

Tips and Tricks:

Ways to Reduce Stress

Stress is often a contributor to chronic inflammation, so learning to manage it is critical to maintaining health. Here are some strategies for reducing stress:

❖ **Meditation and Deep Breathing:**

The mind can be made more at ease and stress levels lowered via the practise of meditation and deep breathing.

Meditation is an ancient practice that can greatly contribute to overall well-being, including controlling inflammation.

Choose a Quiet Place: Find a quiet and peaceful place where you can meditate without distraction.

Set a Goal: Before you begin, set a goal for your meditation. It can be to reduce stress, improve food awareness, or simply relax.

Sit Comfortably: Sit comfortably on a chair or cushion. Keep your back straight to promote concentration.

Focus on Breathing: Start by focusing on your breathing. Breathe slowly and deeply. Notice the inhalation and exhalation without judgment.

Food Awareness: You can also practice meditation while preparing your meals. Be aware of ingredients, textures, and flavors as you cook.

Maintain Regularity: Practice meditation regularly, even for just a few minutes a day. Consistency is key to achieving long-term benefits.

❖ **Deep Breathing to Reduce Stress:**

Deep breathing is a simple but effective technique to reduce stress and promote health. Here's how to do it:

Find a Quiet Moment: Find a quiet place where you can sit or lie down without interruption.

Body Position: Get into a comfortable position. You can sit with your back straight or lie on your back.

Start Breathing: You should close your eyes and concentrate on taking slow, deep breaths. Take a breath in through your nose, and then let it out through your mouth.

Control the Rhythm: Count to four during inhalation and up to six during exhalation. This will help slow the breathing rhythm and reduce stress.

Focus on Breathing: During deep breathing, focus your attention on the sensation of air going in and out of your lungs. Let each breath relax you.

Practice Regularly: Devote a few minutes each day to deep breathing, especially when you feel stressed or anxious.

Combine with Meditation: Deep breathing can be a perfect complement to your meditation practice, helping you relax further.

These meditation and deep breathing strategies can be easily incorporated into daily routines to improve overall well-being and support an anti-inflammatory diet.

Use these techniques before meals to increase food awareness or after a stressful day to relax before dinner.

Regular Physical Activity:

Exercise releases endorphins, which can improve your mood and reduce stress. Reduces chronic inflammation: Regular physical activity can help reduce inflammation in the body, helping to prevent chronic inflammatory diseases.

Supports weight loss: Inflammation can be significantly mitigated by ensuring that your body weight is kept at a healthy level. Cal. can be burned off, and a healthy weight can be maintained with the help of physical exercise.

Improves insulin sensitivity: Insulin sensitivity can be increased through physical activity, which can aid in the prevention of type 2 diabetes.

Promotes mental well-being: Exercise releases endorphins, which can improve mood and reduce stress, helping to control inflammation.

Strategies for Incorporating Exercise into Daily Life:

Choose activities you love: Choose a physical activity you enjoy, whether swimming, walking, dancing, or yoga. This will make it more likely to maintain a routine.

Set realistic goals: Create workout goals that are both attainable and challenging. Begin with manageable objectives, then work your way up in terms of both intensity and length.

Schedule time: Make getting exercise a regular and scheduled part of your day. Find a time when you can engage in physical activity without being disturbed.

Vary your workout: Change the type of activity regularly to avoid habit and prevent overtraining. For example, one day, you can take a walk, another day yoga.

Involve friends: Exercise can be more fun and motivating when you involve friends or family. Organize shared exercise sessions.

Take advantage of breaks: At work, get up from your desk occasionally and do some stretching or a short walk to stimulate circulation.

Use online resources: There are many online resources, such as at-home workout videos, that you can take advantage of to vary your routine.

Training in the Kitchen:

Dance while preparing: Put on music and dance while cooking. It's a fun way to burn Cal.

Iron while you wait: Iron If you have to wait until the food is ready, take advantage of those minutes to do some stretching exercises.

Involve the family: Involve family members in cooking activities, such as mixing or cutting ingredients, so that everyone can be active together.

Always check in with your primary care provider before beginning a new workout routine, but this is especially important if you have any existing medical concerns.

Relaxation Practices:

Relaxation practices are an important complement to an anti-inflammatory lifestyle as they can help reduce stress, promote calm, and improve overall health.

Importance of Relaxation Practices: Relaxation practices are critical to overall health:

Stress Reduction: Chronic stress can increase inflammation in the body. Relaxation practices help reduce stress, thereby reducing the risk of inflammation.

Improving Sleep: Quality sleep is crucial to health. Relaxation practices can improve sleep quality, contributing to optimal recovery.

Improving Mental Well-Being: Relaxation practices, such as meditation or tai chi, can improve mood, reduce anxiety, and promote a calm mind.

Improved Digestion: Stress can negatively affect digestion. Relaxation can improve digestive function.

❖ Strategies for Incorporating Relaxation into Daily Life:

Relaxation practices are an integral part of daily routine:

Find the Right Time: Find a time in your day to engage in relaxation practices. It could be in the morning, during your lunch break, or before bedtime.

Choose the Right Technique: There are a variety of methods available to help one relax, such as meditating, practicing yoga or tai chi, or practicing deep breathing. Pick the option that appeals to you the most.

Create a Relaxing Environment: Find a quiet place where you can practice without distractions. You can light scented candles or listen to relaxing music.

Start with Small Steps: If you are new to the concept of relaxation activities, it is best to begin with shorter sessions, such as five to ten minutes every day, and gradually work your way up to longer sessions.

Involve the Family: Relaxation practices can be shared with the family. Involve your loved ones in family yoga sessions or shared meditation times.

Use Apps and Online Resources: There are numerous apps and videos online that guide you through relaxation practices. Take advantage of these resources for guidance and inspiration.

Relax in the Kitchen: You can also incorporate relaxation practices in the kitchen. As you prepare meals, focus your attention on the sensations, tastes, and smells. This can be a time for relaxation and mindfulness.

❖ Benefits of Relaxation Practices in the Anti-Inflammatory Kitchen:

Improves Digestion: Relaxation before meals can improve digestion and the body's ability to absorb vital nutrients.

Increase Food Awareness: Being mindful while preparing and eating meals can help avoid impulsive food choices and promote an anti-inflammatory diet.

Reduces the Tendency to Eat Emotionally: Relaxation practices can help manage emotions and reduce the tendency to eat in response to stress.

When incorporated into daily life, these relaxation methods can go a long way toward fostering anti-inflammatory health and overall well-being.

Exercise and Sleep

Exercising on a regular basis is an essential component in the management of inflammation. It is essential to locate a physical activity that you take pleasure in, one that maintains your level of activity, and one that can be maintained over time. Sleep is equally important. Here are some suggestions:

Moderate Exercise: Each week, you should aim to do at least 150 minutes of physical exercise at a moderate intensity.

Quality Sleep: Try to sleep at least 7-9 hours a night for optimal rest.

Reducing Screen Time: Reducing the time spent in front of electronic devices before sleeping can improve sleep quality.

Food Diary and Monitoring

Keeping a food diary can help you be aware of your food choices and symptoms. This can be helpful in identifying specific foods that can cause inflammation or discomfort.

Communication with a Health Professional

It's crucial to speak with a health expert before making any major dietary or lifestyle changes. A dietitian or physician can help you develop an anti-inflammatory eating plan tailored to your individual needs.

Healthy Life Habits

Finally, developing healthy lifestyle habits can significantly help reduce chronic inflammation. This includes:

Don't Smoke: If you smoke, seriously consider quitting. Smoking is known to cause inflammation.

Limit Alcohol Consumption: Excessive alcohol consumption can contribute to inflammation, so drink in moderation.

Stress Management: Find healthy ways to deal with stress in your life, such as meditation, art, or time spent with friends and family.

Stress management, exercise, and sleep are important pillars for overall health and keeping chronic inflammation under control.

Chapter 4:

Anti-Inflammatory Breakfast

Spinach and Banana Smoothie

Servings: 1

Ingredients

1 ripe banana (about 4 ounces)

1 C of fresh spinach (about 2 ounces)

4 oz of Greek yogurt

4 oz of almond milk

1 tbsp of chia seeds

1 tsp of honey (optional)

Preparation:

Cut the banana into slices.

In the blender, combine all the ingredients.

Until smooth, blend.

Add honey if you want a touch of additional sweetness.

Pour into a glass and enjoy the smoothie.

Nutritional Plan (per serving):

Cal: about 230 Cal.

Fat: 7g (around 27% of the total Cal.)

PROT: 11g (around 18% of the total Cal.)

Carbs: 36g (around 55% of the total Cal.)

Fiber: 7g (about 28% of total Cal.)

Oats with Fresh Fruit and Walnuts

Servings: 1
Ingredients

1/2 C whole grain oats (about 1.5 ounces)

1 C of coconut milk (roughly 8 ounces)

1/2 C fresh strawberries (roughly 2 ounces)

1/4 C chopped walnuts (about 1.5 ounces)

1 tsp cinnamon powder

Preparation:

In a saucepan, bring the can of coconut milk to a boil.

After adding the oats, the mixture should be cooked for ten to fifteen minutes over medium-low heat. The length of time needed to cook the oats depends on how soft you want the oats to be and how thick you want the mixture to be.

Pour the oats into a bowl.

On top of the oats, sprinkle chopped almonds, cinnamon, and fresh strawberries.

Mix well, then plate.

Nutritional Plan (per serving):

Cal: about 400 Cal.

Fat: 25g (about 56% of total Cal.)

PROT: 10g (about 10% of total Cal.)

Carbs: 40g (about 34% of total Cal.)

Fiber: 8g (about 32% of total Cal.)

Omelette with Herbs and Tomatoes

Servings: 1

Ingredients

2 eggs (about 4 ounces)

2 tbsp of almond milk (about 1.5 ounces)

A handful of fresh chopped parsley (about 0.5 ounces)

1/2 sliced tomato (about 2 ounces)

To taste, add salt and pepper.

Preparation:

In a bowl, whisk together the eggs with the almond milk and the chopped parsley.

A nonstick skillet should be warmed up slowly.

In the pan, pour the egg mixture.

Cook the omelet until it is fully cooked on one side.

The top half of the omelet with tomato slices.

Cook for one minute, or until the omelet is thoroughly cooked, before folding the remaining half over the tomatoes.

To taste, add salt and pepper.

Serve the omelet hot.

Nutritional Plan (per serving):

Cal: about 180 Cal.

Fat: 12g (about 60% of total Cal.)

PROT: 12g (about 27% of total Cal.)

Carbs: 7g (about 13% of total Cal.)

Fiber: 2g (about 4% of total Cal.)

....

Yogurt with Fresh Fruit and Walnuts

Servings: 1
Ingredients

6 oz of Greek yogurt

fresh blueberries, 1/2 C

chopped walnuts, 1/4 C

Honey, one tsp (optional)

Preparation:

In a bowl, pour the Greek yogurt.

Add fresh blueberries and chopped walnuts on top of the yogurt.

If you want a touch of additional sweetness, you can add honey.

Mix well and enjoy this protein- and antioxidant-rich breakfast.

Nutritional Plan (per serving):

Cal: about 350 Cal.

Fat: 20g (about 51% of total Cal.)

PROT: 15g (about 17% of total Cal.)

Carbs: 30g (about 32% of total Cal.)

Fiber: 5g (about 14% of total Cal.)

....

Avocado and Egg Toast

Servings: 1
Ingredients

1 slice of bread made with whole wheat (about 1 ounce)

1/2 ripe avocado (about 2 ounces)

Combine one egg with salt and pepper to taste.

Preparation:

Toast the slice of whole wheat bread until golden brown.

Mash the avocado on a slice of toast.

In a nonstick pan, cook the egg as you prefer (hard-boiled, sunny-side up, etc.).

Lay the cooked egg on top of the crushed avocado.

To taste, add salt and pepper.

Enjoy this toast rich in healthy fats and protein.

Nutritional Plan (per serving):

Cal: about 300 Cal.

Fat: 18g (around 54% of the total Cal.)

PROT: 11g (around 15% of the total Cal.)

Carbs: 26g (around 31% of the total Cal.)

Fiber: 8g (about 28% of total Cal.)

....

Apple Cinnamon Oatmeal

Servings: 1
Ingredients

1/2 C whole grain oats (about 1.5 ounces)

1 C of almond milk (about 8 ounces)

1 apple, diced (about 6 ounces)

1 tsp cinnamon powder

1 tsp of honey (optional)

Preparation:

Bring the almond milk to a boil in a pot.

After adding the oats, the mixture should be cooked for ten to fifteen minutes over medium-low heat. The length of time needed to cook the oats depends on how soft you want the oats to be and how thick you want the mixture to be.

Add diced apple and cinnamon and mix well.

If you want a touch of additional sweetness, you can add honey.

Serve the oats hot.

Nutritional Plan (per serving):

Cal: about 350 Cal.

Fat: 8g (about 21% of total Cal.)

PROT: 7g (about 8% of total Cal.)

Carbs: 65g (about 71% of total Cal.)

Fiber: 11g (about 39% of total Cal.)

Scrambled Eggs with Tomatoes and Spinach

Servings: 1
Ingredients

2 eggs (about 4 ounces)

1/2 C diced tomatoes (roughly 3 ounces)

fresh spinach, 1 C (roughly 2 ounces)

To taste, add salt and pepper.

Preparation:

In a bowl, beat the eggs while adding a pinch of salt and pepper to the mixture.

In a skillet that doesn't need greasing, bring a drop or two of oil up to temperature over medium heat.

Add the chopped tomatoes and fresh spinach to the pan at the point where the spinach is beginning to wilt.

When the eggs are cooked to your preference, pour the beaten eggs over the vegetables and gently stir.

Serve the scrambled eggs hot.

Nutritional Plan (per serving):

Cal: about 250 Cal.

Fat: 16g (about 58% of total Cal.)

PROT: 17g (about 27% of total Cal.)

Carbs: 11g (about 15% of total Cal.)

Fiber: 3g (about 10% of total Cal.)

....

Coconut Mango Smoothie

Servings: 1
Ingredients

50 ml of fresh mango (roughly 2 ounces)

Coconut milk, half a C (roughly 4 ounces)

Coconut yogurt, half a C (4 oz or so)

1 tbsp of flaxseed

1 tbsp grated coconut

1 tsp honey (optional

)

Preparation:

Cut the mango into cubes.

Put all of the ingredients into the blender and mix them together.

Blend up till there are no lumps.

Add honey if you want more sweetness.

Pour into a glass and enjoy this delicious smoothie.

Nutritional Plan (per serving):

Cal: about 350 Cal.

Fat: 20g (about 51% of total Cal.)

Chia Seed Porridge with Fresh Fruit

Servings: 1
Ingredients

Chia seeds, 2 tablespoons

Milk from almonds, 1 C (about 8 ounces)

1/2 C fresh fruit (strawberries, blueberries, or other) (about 4 ounces)

1 tbsp honey or maple syrup (optional)

1 tsp cinnamon powder

A handful of chopped walnuts or almonds (about 1.5 ounces)

Preparation:

In a bowl, mix chia seeds with almond milk and cinnamon.

PROT: 10g (about 11% of total Cal.)

Carbs: 45g (about 38% of total Cal.)

Fiber: 7g (about 25% of total Cal.)

Cover the bowl and place it in the refrigerator for at least two hours, or overnight, if possible, so that the mixture can get more thick.

When serving, add the fresh fruit on top of the chia seed porridge.

If you want a touch of sweetness, you can add honey or maple syrup.

Sprinkle chopped walnuts or almonds on top.

Nutritional Plan (per serving):

Cal: about 350 Cal.

Fat: 20g (about 51% of total Cal.)

PROT: 8g (about 9% of total Cal.)

Carbs: 40g (about 40% of total Cal.)

Fiber: 15g (about 53% of total Cal.)

Avocado and Smoked Salmon Toast

Servings: 1
Ingredients

1 slice of bread made with whole wheat (about 1 ounce)

1/2 ripe avocado (about 2 ounces)

2 thin slices of smoked salmon (about 2 ounces)

Olive oil, 1 teaspoon

1/2 lemon juice

To taste, add salt and pepper.

Preparation:

Toast the slice of whole wheat bread until golden brown.

Mash the avocado on a slice of toast.

Arrange the thin slices of smoked salmon on top of the avocado.

Sprinkle some salt and pepper, as well as lemon juice and olive oil, on top of the salmon.

Enjoy this toast rich in healthy fats and protein.

Nutritional Plan (per serving):

Cal: about 350 Cal.

Fat: 22g (about 57% of total Cal.)

PROT: 18g (about 21% of total Cal.)

Carbs: 25g (about 23% of total Cal.)

Fiber: 9g (about 31% of total Cal.)

....

Detox Green Smoothie

Servings: 1
Ingredients

1 C of fresh spinach (about 2 ounces)

1/2 cucumber, cut into pieces (about 3 ounces)

1 green apple, diced (about 6 ounces)

1/2 banana (about 2 ounces)

1 C of coconut water (about 8 ounces)

1 tbsp of chia seeds

1/2 lemon juice

a tsp of fresh ginger, grated

Preparation:

Put all of the ingredients into the blender and mix them together.

Blend up till there are no lumps.

Enjoy this detoxifying, nutrient-rich smoothie by pouring it into a glass.

Nutritional Plan (per serving):

Cal: about 220 Cal.

Fat: 3g (about 11% of total Cal.)

PROT: 4g (about 7% of total Cal.)

Carbs: 50g (about 82% of total Cal.)

Fiber: 11g (about 39% of total Cal.)

....

Yogurt with Muesli and Dried Fruit

Servings: 1
Ingredients

6 oz of Greek yogurt

1/4 C of muesli (about 1.5 ounces)

1/4 C of dried fruit mixture (walnuts, almonds, hazelnuts, etc.) (about 1.5 ounces)

1 tbsp honey or maple syrup (optional)

1/2 sliced banana (about 2 ounces)

Preparation:

In a bowl, pour the Greek yogurt.

Sprinkle the muesli and dried fruit mixture on top of the yogurt.

If you want a touch of sweetness, you can add honey or maple syrup.

Lay the banana slices on top.

Nutritional Plan (per serving):

Cal: about 380 Cal.

Fat: 18g (about 42% of total Cal.)

PROT: 16g (about 17% of total Cal.)

Carbs: 44g (about 41% of total Cal.)

Fiber: 6g (about 16% of total Cal.)

....

Peanut Butter and Banana Sandwiches

Servings: 1
Ingredients

2 pieces of bread made with whole wheat (about 2 ounces)

2 tbsp of natural peanut butter (about 2 ounces)

1 banana, sliced (about 4 ounces)

Preparation:

Toast some whole-grain bread.

Slice of bread with peanut butter on it.

Arrange the banana slices in a pretty pattern on top of the peanut butter.

Add the second slice of toast on top.

Enjoy this protein- and potassium-rich sandwich.

Nutritional Plan (per serving):

Cal: about 400 Cal.

Fat: 16g (about 36% of total Cal.)

PROT: 11g (about 11% of total Cal.)

Carbs: 61g (about 53% of total Cal.)

Fiber: 9g (about 24% of total Cal.)

....

Oats with Berries and Flaxseed

Servings: 1
Ingredients

1/2 C whole grain oats (about 1.5 ounces)

1 C of almond milk (about 8 ounces)

half a cup of a variety of berries (such as strawberries, blueberries, and raspberries, among others) (about 4 ounces)

1 tbsp of flaxseed

1 tbsp sliced almonds (about 0.5 ounces)

1 tsp of honey (optional)

Preparation:

To make almond milk, bring the almond milk to a boil in a saucepan.

After adding the oats, the mixture should be cooked for ten to fifteen minutes over medium-low heat. The length of time needed to cook the oats depends on how soft you want the oats to be and how thick you want the mixture to be.

Pour the cooked oats into a bowl.

Sprinkle the berries, flax seeds, and sliced almonds over the oats.

If you want a touch of sweetness, you can add honey.

Mix well and enjoy this nutritious breakfast.

Nutritional Plan (per serving):

Cal: about 350 Cal.

Fat: 12g (about 31% of total Cal.)

PROT: 10g (about 11% of total Cal.)

Carbs: 52g (about 58% of total Cal.)

Fiber: 11g (about 40% of total Cal.)

....

Oat and Banana Pancakes

Servings: 2
Ingredients

1 C of oatmeal (about 3 ounces)

1 ripe banana

2 eggs

Almond milk, half a C (about 4 ounces)

1 tsp ground cinnamon

Vanilla extract, 1 teaspoon

Honey, one tsp (optional)

Preparation:
Oatmeal, banana, eggs, almond milk, cinnamon, and vanilla extract should all be combined in a blender.

Until smooth, blend.

A nonstick pan that has been lightly coated with olive oil is heated over medium heat.

To create pancakes of the required size, pour the batter.

Pancakes should be cooked until both sides are golden brown.

Before serving, drizzle honey on top of the pancakes if you'd like a bit more sweetness.

Nutritional Plan (per serving):

Cal: about 300 Cal.

Fat: 8g (around 24% of the total Cal.)

PROT: 11g (around 15% of the total Cal.)

Carbs: 52g (approximately 61% of total Cal.)

Fiber: 7g (about 23% of total Cal.)

Cocoa and Banana Smoothie

Servings: 1
Ingredients

1 ripe banana (about 4 ounces)

1 tbsp unsweetened cocoa powder

1/2 C of almond milk (about 4 ounces)

1 tbsp almond butter (about 1 ounce)

1 tbsp of chia seeds

1 tsp of honey (optional)

Preparation:

In the blender, combine all the ingredients.

Until smooth, blend.

If you want a touch of sweetness, you can add honey.

Pour into a glass and enjoy this chocolate banana smoothie.

Nutritional Plan (per serving):

Cal: about 350 Cal.

Fat: 14g (around 36% of the total Cal.)

PROT: 8g (around 9% of the total Cal.)

Carbs: 53g (around 55% of the total Cal.)

Fiber: 10g (about 35% of total Cal.)

....

Omelette with Herbs and Tomatoes

Servings: 1
Ingredients

2 eggs (about 4 ounces)

1/2 tomato, diced (about 3 ounces)

A handful of fresh spinach (about 2 ounces)

1 tbsp of freshly chopped herbs (parsley, basil, thyme, etc.).

To taste, add salt and pepper.

1 tsp of olive oil

Preparation:

In a bowl, beat the eggs while adding a pinch of salt and pepper to the mixture.

Olive oil should be warmed up in a skillet that won't stick to the pan over medium heat.

After the spinach has become limp, stir in the tomato and continue it boil for two to three minutes.

After adding the fresh herbs, pour the beaten eggs over the vegetables.

Cook until the omelet is cooked to your taste.

Serve the omelet hot.

Nutritional Plan (per serving):

Cal: about 220 Cal.

Fat: 14g (about 57% of total Cal.)

PROT: 14g (about 25% of total Cal.)

Carbs: 10g (about 18% of total Cal.)

Fiber: 3g (about 11% of total Cal.)

....

Quinoa Porridge and Dried Fruit

Servings: 1
Ingredients

1/2 C of raw quinoa (about 3 ounces)

1 C of almond milk (about 8 ounces)

1/4 C of dried fruit mix (walnuts, almonds, raisins, etc.) (about 1.5 ounces)

1 tsp cinnamon powder

1 tsp honey or maple syrup (optional)

Preparation:

Rinse the quinoa well under running water.

Bring the almond milk to a boil in a pot.

After the mixture has reached the appropriate consistency and the quinoa has been cooked, add the cinnamon and continue to simmer over low heat for an additional fifteen to twenty minutes.

Pour the porridge into a bowl.

Sprinkle the dried fruit mix over the porridge.

If you want a touch of sweetness, you can add honey or maple syrup.

Mix well and enjoy this nutritious porridge.

Nutritional Plan (per serving):

Cal: about 400 Cal.

Fat: 14g (about 32% of total Cal.)

PROT: 10g (about 10% of total Cal.)

Carbs: 60g (about 58% of total Cal.)

Fiber: 7g (about 25% of total Cal.)

....

Egg and Spinach Toast

Servings: 1
Ingredients
1 slice of whole wheat bread (about 1 ounce)

2 eggs (about 4 ounces)

1 C of fresh spinach (about 2 ounces)

To taste, add salt and pepper.

Olive oil, 1 teaspoon

Preparation:

The whole wheat bread slice has been toasted.

In a pan that won't stick, olive oil should be warmed up over a medium heat setting.

After heating the skillet for two to three minutes, fresh spinach should be added and cooked until it has become wilted.

In a basin, beat the eggs before adding them to the pan with the spinach.

Gently stir the eggs over medium heat until they are cooked to your liking.

Place a slice of toast on top of the scrambled eggs.

To taste, add salt and pepper.

Serve toast hot.

Nutritional Plan (per serving):

Cal: about 320 Cal.

Fat: 16g (about 45% of total Cal.)

PROT: 17g (about 21% of total Cal.)

Carbs: 26g (about 34% of total Cal.)

Fiber: 5g (about 15% of total Cal.)

Apple Cinnamon Muffins

Servings: 1 muffin
Ingredients

Oatmeal, 1 C (about 3 ounces)

A half-cup of almond flour (about 2 ounces)

1 tsp ground cinnamon

one tbsp of baking powder

an apple, grated, in 1/4 C (about 1.5 ounces)

1 egg

a quarter C of almond milk (about 2 ounces)

the an a

Honey, one tsp (optional)

Preparation:

Put ramekins in a muffin tin and preheat the oven to 180 degrees Celsius (350 degrees Fahrenheit).

In a bowl, mix together the flour made from almonds and oatmeal, as well as the baking powder and cinnamon.

Another bowl should be used to beat the egg, and then the grated apple, almond milk, olive oil, and honey should be mixed together (if you wish to sweeten).

After adding the wet ingredients to the dry ingredients in the bowl, make sure the wet ingredients are properly combined.

Spoon the batter into the muffin tins, filling them up to three-quarters of the way.

Bake the muffins for 20 to 25 minutes or until they have a golden brown color all the way through and are fully cooked.

Before serving, allow to cool.

Nutrition Plan (per muffin):

Cal: about 160 Cal.

Fat: 9g (about 50% of total Cal.)

PROT: 5g (about 12% of total Cal.)

Carbs: 16g (about 38% of total Cal.)

Fiber: 3g (about 18% of total Cal.)

....

Avocado and Spinach Smoothie

Servings: 1
Ingredients

1/2 ripe avocado (about 2 ounces)

1 C of fresh spinach (about 2 ounces)

1/2 banana (about 2 ounces)

1 C of water (about 8 ounces)

1 tbsp of chia seeds

Juice of 1/2 lemon

1 tsp of honey (optional)

Preparation:

Put all of the ingredients into the blender and mix them together.

Blend up till there are no lumps.

You can add honey to give it a little more sweetness if you want to.

This smoothie is loaded with nutritious fats and vegetables, so pour it into a glass and drink it right away.

Nutritional Plan (per serving):

Cal: about 250 Cal.

Fat: 15g (about 54% of total Cal.)

PROT: 5g (about 8% of total Cal.)

Carbs: 28g (about 38% of total Cal.)

Fiber: 9g (about 32% of total Cal.)

Coconut Muesli with Yogurt and Fresh Fruit

Servings: 1
Ingredients

1/2 C coconut muesli (about 2 ounces)

1/2 C of Greek yogurt (about 4 ounces)

1/2 C fresh fruit (strawberries, blueberries, kiwi, etc.) (about 4 ounces)

1 tbsp chopped walnuts or almonds (about 0.5 ounces)

1 tsp honey or maple syrup (optional)

Preparation:

In a bowl, mix coconut muesli and Greek yogurt.

Sprinkle fresh fruit on top of the muesli.

Add chopped walnuts or almonds.

If you want a touch of sweetness, you can add honey or maple syrup.

Mix well and enjoy this fresh and nutritious muesli.

Nutritional Plan (per serving):

Cal: about 300 Cal.

Fat: 9g (about 27% of total Cal.)

PROT: 12g (about 16% of total Cal.)

Carbs: 47g (about 57% of total Cal.)

Fiber: 6g (about 21% of total Cal.)

Amaranth Porridge with Fresh Fruit

Servings: 1
Ingredients

1/2 C raw amaranth (about 3 ounces)

1 C of almond milk (about 8 ounces)

1/2 C of fresh fruit of your choice (strawberries, blueberries, pears, etc.) (about 4 ounces)

1 tbsp chopped walnuts (about 0.5 ounces)

1 tsp honey or maple syrup (optional)

Preparation:

In a pot, bring the almond milk all the way up to a boil.

Amaranth should be added after the heat has been lowered.

Amaranth should be cooked for 20 to 25

minutes or until it has absorbed the liquid and reached the desired tenderness.

Pour the porridge into a bowl.

Sprinkle fresh fruit and chopped nuts over the porridge.

If you want a touch of sweetness, you can add honey or maple syrup.

Mix well and enjoy this protein- and fiber-rich breakfast.

Nutritional Plan (per serving):

Cal: about 350 Cal.

Fat: 9g (about 23% of total Cal.)

PROT: 10g (about 11% of total Cal.)

Carbs: 58g (about 66% of total Cal.)

Fiber: 9g (about 32% of total Cal.)

....

Vegetable Frittata with Avocado

Servings: 1
Ingredients

2 eggs (about 4 ounces)

1/2 ripe avocado (about 2 ounces)

1/4 diced red bell pepper (about 1.5 ounces)

1/4 diced red onion (about 1.5 ounces)

To taste, add salt and pepper.

Olive oil, 1 teaspoon

Preparation:

In a pan that won't stick, olive oil should be warmed up over a medium heat setting.

After adding the bell pepper and onion, continue to simmer the mixture for

another three to four minutes or until the vegetables are tender.

In a bowl, beat the eggs while adding a pinch of salt and pepper to the mixture.

Pour the eggs, which have been beaten, on top of the vegetables in the pan.

The omelet should be cooked to your liking over medium heat while being gently stirred.

Serve the omelet warm with sliced avocado on top.

Nutritional Plan (per serving):

Cal: about 350 Cal.

Fat: 24g (around 62% of the total Cal.)

PROT: 13g (around 15% of the total Cal.)

Carbs: 20g (around 23% of the total Cal.)

Fiber: 9g (about 32% of total Cal.)

....

Pineapple Ginger Smoothie

Servings: 1
Ingredients

1/2 C fresh pineapple (roughly 4 ounces)

1/2 banana (roughly 2 ounces)

Freshly grated ginger, half a teaspoon

1 C of coconut water (about 8 ounces)

1 tbsp of chia seeds

Juice of 1/2 lemon

1 tsp of honey (optional)

Preparation:

Put all of the ingredients into the blender and mix them together.

Blend up till there are no lumps.

If you want a touch of sweetness, you can add honey.

Pour into a glass and enjoy this tropical, anti-inflammatory smoothie.

Nutritional Plan (per serving):

Cal: about 220 Cal.

Fat: 5g (about 20% of total Cal.)

PROT: 5g (about 9% of total Cal.)

Carbs: 42g (about 71% of total Cal.)

Fiber: 8g (about 27% of total Cal.)

Oatmeal Pancakes with Berries

Servings: 2
Ingredients

1 C instant oatmeal

Almond milk, half a cup

2 tsp of honey and 1 egg (optional)

Fresh or frozen berries for garnish

Preparation:

In a bowl, mix the rolled oats, almond milk, and egg together. Honey is a great addition to any dish that needs just a touch of sweetness.

The batter for the pancakes should be poured onto a nonstick frying pan that has been heated to a medium setting.

Cook them until bubbles start to develop on the surface, then flip them over and continue cooking until the other side is golden brown.

Warm the pancakes and serve them alongside the berries.

Nutritional Plan (per serving):

Cal: about 250 Cal.

Fat: 6g (around 21% of the total Cal.)

PROT: 10g (around 15% of the total Cal.)

Carbs: 42g (around 64% of the total Cal.)

Fiber: 5g (about 20% of total Cal.)

Yogurt with Blueberries and Walnuts

2 tbsp of walnuts, chopped

Honey, one tsp (optional)

Servings: 1
Ingredients

Preparation:

1 C of Greek yogurt

1/2 C blueberries, either fresh or frozen

In a bowl, put the Greek yogurt.

Add blueberries and chopped walnuts.

If you want a touch of sweetness, you can add honey.

Mix well and serve.

Nutritional Plan (per serving):

Cal: about 300 Cal.

Fat: 16g (about 48% of total Cal.)

PROT: 15g (about 20% of total Cal.)

Carbs: 29g (about 32% of total Cal.)

Fiber: 5g (about 17% of total Cal.)

....

Frittata with Spinach and Tomatoes

Servings: 2
Ingredients

4 eggs

1 C of fresh spinach

1 diced tomato

To taste, add salt and pepper.

Olive oil, 1 teaspoon

Preparation:

In a bowl, beat the eggs while adding a pinch of salt and pepper to the mixture.

Olive oil should be warmed up in a skillet that won't stick to the pan over medium heat.

Cook for a few minutes, or until the spinach wilts, after adding the spinach and tomatoes.

When the omelet is cooked to your preference, pour the beaten eggs over the vegetables.

Divide the omelet into two portions and serve hot.

Nutritional Plan (per serving):

Cal: about 170 Cal.

Fat: 11g (about 58% of total Cal.)

PROT: 13g (about 31% of total Cal.)

Carbs: 7g (about 11% of total Cal.)

Fiber: 2g (about 7% of total Cal.)

....

Avocado Toast with Egg and Dried Tomatoes

Servings: 1
Ingredients

1 whole wheat piece of bread

ripe avocado, half

1 egg

2-3 chopped sun-dried tomatoes in oil

To taste, add salt and pepper.

chile peppers, red (optional)

For garnish, use fresh herbs (basil, parsley).

Preparation:

Toast the slice of whole wheat bread.

Mash the avocado on the slice of toast.

In a nonstick skillet, prepare the egg as you prefer (hard-boiled, sunny-side up, scrambled).

Place the egg on top of the crushed avocado.

Sprinkle chopped sun-dried tomatoes over the egg.

Add some salt, pepper, and crushed red pepper flakes if you like things on the spicy side.

Garnish with fresh herbs after heating, and serve hot.

Nutritional Plan (per serving):

Cal: about 350 Cal.

Fat: 24g (about 61% of total Cal.)

PROT: 11g (about 12% of total Cal.)

Carbs: 27g (about 27% of total Cal.)

Fiber: 10g (about 36% of total Cal.)

....

Quinoa Porridge with Fresh Fruit and Walnuts

Servings: 2
Ingredients

1 C of raw quinoa

2 C of almond milk

1 apple, diced

chopped walnuts, 1/4 cup

1 cinnamon stick

Honey or maple syrup (optional)

Preparation:

Rinse the quinoa well under cold water.

In a saucepan, quinoa and almond milk are mixed together. After it has to a boil, reduce the heat, cover the pot, and let the quinoa simmer for 15–20 minutes, or until it has reached the desired consistency.

The cooked quinoa should be combined with the diced apple, chopped walnuts, and cinnamon. Mix thoroughly.

You can include honey or maple syrup to provide a hint of sweetness.

If desired, top the hot porridge with more fresh fruit before serving.

Nutritional Plan (per serving):
Cal: about 400 Cal.

Fat: 13g (about 29% of total Cal.)

PROT: 10g (about 10% of total Cal.)

Carbs: 62g (about 61% of total Cal.)

Fiber: 8g (about 32% of total Cal.)

Banana and Spinach Smoothie with Chia Seeds

Servings: 1
Ingredients

1 ripe banana

1 handful of fresh spinach

1 C of almond milk without sugar

Chia seeds, 1 tbsp

1 tsp of maple syrup or honey (optional)

Ice (optional)

Preparation:

Put the banana, spinach, almond milk, and chia seeds in a high-power blender.

Add honey or maple syrup if you want extra sweetness.

If you prefer your smoothie cooler, you can add ice.

Combine all of the ingredients until they are smooth.

After pouring the smoothie into a glass, you can start enjoying it right away.

Nutritional Plan (per serving):

Cal: about 300 Cal.

Fat: 8g (about 24% of total Cal.)

PROT: 6g (about 8% of total Cal.)

Carbs: 55g (about 68% of total Cal.)

Fiber: 10g (about 34% of total Cal.)

Coconut Parfait with Berries

Servings: 2
Ingredients

1 C unsweetened coconut yogurt

1 C of berries, all kinds (strawberries, blueberries, blackberries)

1/2 C of granola without sugar

2 tbsp of dehydrated coconut

Honey or maple syrup (optional)

Preparation:

Start with a layer of coconut yogurt at the bottom of two glasses or bowls.

Add a layer of mixed berries.

Sprinkle some sugar-free granola on top of the berries.

Continue alternating layers of yogurt, berries, and granola until the glasses are full.

Top with dehydrated coconut and, if desired, a drizzle of honey or maple syrup for sweetness.

Serve immediately or refrigerate for a fresh, ready-to-eat breakfast in the morning.

Nutritional Plan (per serving):

Cal: about 350 Cal.

Baked C of Oats with Apple and Cinnamon

Servings: 1
Ingredients

1/2 C instant oats

1 peeled and diced apple

1/2 tsp cinnamon

1 tbsp chopped walnuts

1 tbsp honey or maple syrup (optional)

1 C of unsweetened almond milk

Preparation:

The oven temperature is set at 350°F (180°C).

Combine quick oats, apple chunks, and cinnamon in a bowl.

Fat: 14g (around 36% of the total Cal.)

PROT: 8g (around 9% of the total Cal.)

Carbs: 49g (around 55% of the total Cal.)

Fiber: 7g (about 25% of total Cal.)

If you want a hint of sweetness, mix in some chopped almonds and honey or maple syrup.

Transfer the mixture to a heat-resistant C or oven/microwave container.

Pour the almond milk over the oats and stir gently.

The oats should be cooked, and the surface should be golden brown after 25 to 30 minutes of baking.

Take the cooked oats out of the oven, let them cool a little, and then enjoy a steaming cup.

Nutritional Plan (per serving):

Cal: about 350 Cal.

Fat: 8g (about 21% of total Cal.)

PROT: 8g (about 9% of total Cal.)

Carbs: 63g (about 70% of total Cal.)

Fiber: 9g (about 32% of total Cal.)

....

Cocoa and Banana Smoothie Bowl

Servings: 1
Ingredients

one ripe banana

Unsweetened cocoa powder, 2 tablespoons

12 C almond milk without sugar

1/4 C almond butter

Muesli with no additional sugar in 1/4 cup

Fresh fruit of your choice (strawberries, blueberries, bananas) for garnish

Preparation:

In a high-power blender, combine the banana, cocoa powder, almond milk, and almond butter.

Blend until creamy and smooth.

The mixture should be poured into a bowl.

Sprinkle sugar-free muesli over the surface.

Garnish with the fresh fruit of your choice.

Serve immediately, and enjoy your cocoa and banana smoothie bowl.

Nutritional Plan (per serving):

Cal: about 400 Cal.

Fat: 15g (about 34% of total Cal.)

PROT: 9g (about 9% of total Cal.)

Carbs: 65g (about 57% of total Cal.)

Fiber: 12g (about 40% of total Cal.)

....

Avocado Toast with Pesto Eggs

Servings: 2
Ingredients

2 slices of whole wheat bread

1 ripe avocado

2 eggs

2 tbsp basil pesto (without cheese)

To taste, add salt and pepper.

cherry tomatoes as an ornament (optional)

garnished with fresh basil (optional)

Preparation:

Toast slices of whole wheat bread.

Meanwhile, prepare the eggs as you prefer (sunny-side up, scrambled, poached, etc.).

After mashing the avocado in a bowl, season it with a little bit of salt and pepper.

On the toasted bread slices, spread the mashed avocado.

On top of the avocado, place the cooked eggs.

Each slice of bread should have a dollop of basil pesto on it.

If preferred, garnish with fresh basil and cherry tomatoes.

Serve hot pesto eggs with avocado toast.

Nutritional Plan (per serving):

Cal: about 350 Cal.

Fat: 19g (around 49% of the total Cal.)

PROT: 13g (around 15% of the total Cal.)

Carbs: 32g (about 36% of the total Cal.))

Fiber: 8g (about 27% of total Cal.)

....

CHAPTER 5

Nutritious Lunches

Midday meals should be nutritious and provide the energy needed for the afternoon.

....

Quinoa Salad with Chickpeas and Vegetables

Servings: 2
Ingredients

8 oz of cooked quinoa

8 oz cooked chickpeas (rinsed and drained)

8 oz cherry tomatoes cut in half

8 oz cucumber, diced

8 oz of red bell pepper, thinly sliced

2 tbsp of extra virgin olive oil and 2 oz of chopped fresh basil leaves

Lemon juice from one

To taste, add salt and pepper.

Preparation:

It is recommended that the quinoa, chickpeas, cherry tomatoes, cucumber, and red bell pepper be mixed together in a sizable bowl.

In a small bowl, combine the ingredients for a vinaigrette as follows: olive oil, lemon juice, basil, salt, and pepper.

After adding the vinaigrette, gently toss the salad.

Serve quinoa salad as a main meal or side dish.

Nutritional Plan (per serving):

Cal: about 400 Cal.

Fat: 14g (around 31% of the total Cal.)

PROT: 14g (around 14% of the total Cal.)

Carbs: 57g (around 55% of the total Cal.)

Fiber: 12g (about 32% of total Cal.)

....

Baked Salmon with Asparagus and Sweet Potatoes

Servings: 2
Ingredients

2 fillets of salmon (roughly 5 oz each)

1 bunch of asparagus, hard parts removed

2 sweet potatoes, thinly sliced

Olive oil extra virgin, 2 tablespoons

1 tsp paprika sweet

To taste, add salt and pepper.

Lime as a garnish

Preparation:

Put the oven temperature to 400 degrees Fahrenheit (200 degrees Celsius).

Prepare a baking dish for the sweet potato slices and asparagus spears by arranging them in the dish.

Add salt, pepper, sweet paprika, and half the olive oil to season. Stir thoroughly.

Over the vegetables, place the salmon fillets.

Before seasoning the salmon, add the remaining olive oil to a small bowl and then whisk in the salt, pepper, and lemon juice.

Cook the fish and sweet potatoes in the oven for 15 to 20 minutes or until they reach an internal temperature of 145 degrees Fahrenheit.

Serve heated sweet potatoes and asparagus with the fish.

Nutritional Plan (per serving):
Cal: about 450 Cal.

Fat: 18g (about 36% of total Cal.)

PROT: 35g (about 31% of total Cal.)

Carbs: 35g (about 33% of total Cal.)

Fiber: 7g (about 20% of total Cal.)

Chicken Curry Salad with Almonds

Servings: 2
Ingredients

8 oz cooked and diced chicken breast

2 tbsp sliced almonds

2 C of mixed lettuce

1/2 green apple, diced

2 tbsp of Greek yogurt

1 tsp curry powder

The juice of 1/2 lemon

To taste, add salt and pepper.

Preparation:

Diced cooked chicken breast, sliced almonds, mixed lettuce, and diced green apple are all combined in a big bowl.

Greek yogurt, curry powder, lemon juice, salt, and pepper should be combined in a small bowl to make a curry vinaigrette.

After pouring on the vinaigrette, give the salad a gentle toss to ensure that all of the components are evenly coated.

Serve chicken curry salad as a main meal.

Nutritional Plan (per serving):

Cal: about 350 Cal.

Fat: 10g (about 26% of total Cal.)

PROT: 30g (about 34% of total Cal.)

Carbs: 30g (about 40% of total Cal.)

Fiber: 6g (about 24% of total Cal.)

Red Lentil and Tomato Soup

Servings: 2
Ingredients

1 C dried red lentils

1 C peeled tomatoes, chopped

1/2 onion, chopped finely

2 minced garlic cloves

4 C of veggie stock

one tsp of turmeric powder

1 tsp of ground cumin

To taste, add salt and pepper.

Garnishing with fresh parsley (optional)

Preparation:

Rinse red lentils under running water until the water is clear.

First, bring a pot of vegetable broth up to temperature, then add the onion and garlic that have been chopped. They need to be cooked till the transparency is reached.

Add the remaining vegetable broth, tomatoes that have been chopped and skinned, red lentils that have been washed, turmeric, cumin, and salt and pepper to taste.

After the soup has reached a full boil, turn the heat down to low, cover, and continue to simmer for 20 to 25 minutes or until the lentils are completely cooked.

Serve the red lentil and tomato soup hot, garnishing with fresh parsley if desired.

Nutritional Plan (per serving):

Cal: about 320 Cal.

Fat: 1g (about 3% of total Cal.)

PROT: 16g (about 20% of total Cal.)

Carbs: 60g (about 77% of total Cal.)

Fiber: 18g (about 72% of total Cal.)

Quinoa Salad with Roasted Beets and Almonds

Ingredients (for 2 servings):

2 oz (about 1/2 cup) of quinoa

8 oz (approximately 2 small) chopped and peeled beets

1/4 C of sliced almonds, 1 oz.

Extra virgin olive oil, 1 1/2 tablespoons

lemon juice from one

Honey, one tsp (optional)

To taste, add salt and black pepper.

Garnishing with fresh parsley

Preparation:

Put the oven temperature to 400 degrees Fahrenheit (200 degrees Celsius).

In a saucepan, prepare the quinoa in accordance with the instructions provided on the packaging. After it has been cooked, set it aside.

Be sure to season the beet cubes with salt, pepper, and a half tablespoon of olive oil before spreading them out on a baking sheet. Bake the beets for 20 to 25 minutes or until they have reached the desired tenderness and are beginning to caramelize. The cooking process involves intermittent stirring.

A skillet that does not adhere to the food should be used to lightly toast sliced almonds over medium heat. Place each one on its own plate and wait for it to get cool.

Vinaigrette can be prepared by combining the remaining olive oil, lemon juice, honey (if you want the dish to have a touch of sweetness), salt, and pepper in a small bowl. The mixture can then be stirred.

In a large bowl, combine the quinoa that has been cooked, the roasted beets, and the toasted almonds.

Vinaigrette should be drizzled over the salad, and then the salad should be gently mixed to ensure that the contents are evenly distributed.

Garnish the salad with parsley that has been freshly cut, and serve it either as a main meal or a side dish.

Nutritional Plan (per serving):

Cal: about 300 Cal.

Fat: 15g (about 45% of total Cal.)

PROT: 7g (about 10% of total Cal.)

Carbs: 35g (about 45% of total Cal.)

Fiber: 6g (about 20% of total Cal.)

Grilled Salmon with Curry and Mango Sauce

Servings: 2
Ingredients: (for 2

2 salmon fillets (4 oz each)

1 mango, diced after being peeled

1 chopped red bell pepper

Curry powder, 1 teaspoon

Extra virgin olive oil, 1 teaspoon

lemon juice from one

To taste, add salt and pepper.

Chopped fresh parsley for garnish

Preparation:

Set the grill's temperature to medium-high.

In a bowl, all of the following ingredients should be mixed together: mango, red bell pepper, olive oil, lemon juice, curry powder, salt, and pepper. This will be the sauce that goes with the fish.

Spraying the salmon fillets with olive oil will prevent them from sticking to the grill and will also add flavor.

It is recommended that you grill the salmon for around four to five minutes per side or until the fish is cooked through and has developed a light browning.

Once cooked, pour the curry and mango sauce over the grilled salmon.

Sprinkle with freshly chopped parsley for a fresh touch.

Serve hot, possibly with a side of quinoa or lush green veggies.

Nutritional Plan (per serving):

Cal: about 320 Cal.

Fat: 12g (about 34% of total Cal.)

PROT: 32g (about 38% of total Cal.)

Carbs: 23g (about 28% of total Cal.)

Fiber: 4g (about 16% of total Cal.)

....

Salmon Tacos with Avocado Sauce

Servings: 2
Ingredients

8 oz salmon fillets, skinless

1 ripe avocado

1/4 C coarsely chopped red onion

diced 1/4 C tomato

1 lemon juice and 1/4 C of chopped fresh coriander

4 tortillas, either corn or wheat

To taste, add salt and pepper.

Extra virgin olive oil, 1 tablespoon

Preparation:

Olive oil should be heated in a skillet that does not stick by using medium-high heat.

Prepare the salmon fillets by searing them on both sides for three to four minutes or until the fish readily flakes apart. Salt and pepper should be added to taste.

While the salmon is cooking, prepare the avocado sauce by mashing the ripe avocado in a bowl and blending it with the red onion, tomato, cilantro, and lemon juice. While the avocado sauce is cooking, serve the salmon. Salt and pepper should be added to taste.

In a microwave or frying pan, warm the tortillas.

Once ready, flake the cooked salmon into smaller pieces.

Fill the tortillas with the flaked salmon and avocado salsa.

Serve salmon tacos with avocado salsa as a main meal.

Nutritional Plan (per serving):
Cal: about 380 Cal.

Fat: 21g (around 50% of total Cal.)

PROT: 28g (about 29% of total Cal.)

Carbs: 28g (about 21% of total Cal.)

Fiber: 9g (about 28% of total Cal.)

Quinoa Salad with Grilled Vegetables and Feta Cheese

Servings: 2
Ingredients

8 oz of cooked quinoa

4 oz feta cheese, crumbled

4 oz zucchini, thinly sliced and grilled

4 oz cherry tomatoes, cut in half

2 oz red onion, finely chopped

Olive oil extra virgin, 2 tablespoons

1 tsp dried oregano,

2 tbsp balsamic vinegar

To taste, add salt and pepper.

Preparation:

Combine cooked quinoa, feta cheese crumbles, grilled zucchini, cherry tomato halves, and red onion in a big bowl.

To make a vinaigrette, add dried oregano, balsamic vinegar, salt, and pepper in a small bowl, along with olive oil and balsamic vinegar.

To ensure that each component of the quinoa salad has a uniform coating, simply drizzle the vinaigrette over the salad.

Serve quinoa salad with grilled vegetables and feta as a main meal or side dish.

Nutritional Plan (per serving):

Cal: about 450 Cal.

Fat: 22g (about 44% of total Cal.)

PROT: 13g (around 12% of the total Cal.)

Carbs: 50g (about 44% of total Cal.)

Fiber: 7g (about 20% of total Cal.)

....

Grilled Chicken with Lemon and Capers Sauce

Servings: 2
Ingredients

12 oz chicken breast, skinless

2 tbsp capers, rinsed

2 minced garlic cloves

Lemon juice from one

1 tbsp of extra virgin olive oil,

plus 2 tsp of chopped fresh parsley

To taste, add salt and pepper.

Preparation:

Garlic that has been minced, capers, fresh parsley, lemon juice, olive oil, salt, and pepper should all be combined in a bowl to produce a marinade.

Before pouring any more of the marinade, check to see that the chicken breasts have received an even coating of it. Marinating requires at least half an hour in the refrigerator, so start that now.

Bring a grill or a skillet up to a temperature that is somewhere between medium and high.

After around 6 to 8 minutes per side on the grill, the chicken should be cooked through completely.

As a main course, serve grilled chicken with a lemon caper sauce.

Nutritional Plan (per serving):

Cal: about 290 Cal.

Fat: 9g (about 28% of total Cal.)

PROT: 41g (around 57% of the total Cal.)

Carbs: 8g (about 15% of total Cal.)

Fiber: 2g (about 7% of total Cal.)

....

Buckwheat Bowl with Roasted Vegetables

Servings: 2
Ingredients

4 oz raw buckwheat

8 oz broccoli, divided into florets

8 oz carrots, thinly sliced

8 oz cauliflower, divided into florets

Extra virgin olive oil, 1 tablespoon

smoked paprika, 1 teaspoon

To taste, add salt and pepper.

4 tbsp hummus

Toasted sesame seeds for garnish (optional)

Preparation:

Buckwheat should be prepared as directed on the packet. Place it aside after cooking.

Put the oven temperature to 400 degrees Fahrenheit (200 degrees Celsius).

In a baking dish, you should put florets of cauliflower and broccoli, as well as slices of carrot and carrot florets. For seasoning, add salt, pepper, smoked paprika, and olive oil. Season with salt and pepper. Combine in great detail.

The vegetables should be cooked in an oven that has been prepared for 20 to 25 minutes or until they have reached the desired consistency of being tender while still having a light browning.

To assemble the bowl, spread the cooked buckwheat on the plates and add the roasted vegetables.

Top with spoonfuls of hummus and toasted sesame seeds if desired.

Nutritional Plan (per serving):

Cal: about 380 Cal.

Fat: 11g (about 26% of total Cal.)

PROT: 12g (around 12% of the total Cal.)

Carbs: 64g (about 62% of total Cal.)

Fiber: 10g (about 25% of total Cal.)

Spinach Salad with Grilled Chicken and Almonds

Servings: 2
Ingredients

8 oz grilled chicken breast, thinly sliced

6 oz of fresh spinach

2 oz sliced almonds

2 tbsp feta cheese, crumbled

Olive oil extra virgin, 2 tablespoons

Balsamic vinegar, two tablespoons

Honey, one teaspoon

To taste, add salt and pepper.

Preparation:

Place in a large bowl sliced almonds, crumbled feta cheese, fresh spinach, and thinly sliced grilled chicken breasts.

To make a vinaigrette, combine honey, balsamic vinegar, salt, and pepper in a small basin along with olive oil and balsamic vinegar.

Vinaigrette should be drizzled over the spinach salad so that all of the components are evenly coated with the dressing.

Serve spinach salad with grilled chicken and almonds as a main meal.

Nutritional Plan (per serving):

Cal: about 410 Cal.

Fat: 28g (about 61% of total Cal.)

PROT: 32g (about 31% of total Cal.)

Carbs: 17g (about 8% of total Cal.)

Fiber: 4g (about 11% of total Cal.)

Curried Tofu Wrap with Hummus

Servings: 2
Ingredients

8 oz tofu, cut into thin strips

4 oz of hummus

4 whole wheat tortillas

curry powder, 1 teaspoon

a half-teaspoon of sweet paprika

Extra virgin olive oil, 1 tablespoon

To taste, add salt and pepper.

Vegetables of your choice for the filling (e.g., lettuce, tomatoes, cucumbers)

Preparation:

It is best to bring the olive oil to temperature in a frying pan set over medium-high heat.

After adding the tofu strips, season them with curry powder, sweet paprika, black pepper, and salt. Cook each side for four to five minutes or until it reaches a golden brown color.

Both a skillet and a microwave are suitable heating methods for tortillas produced from whole wheat.

To assemble the wraps, spread some hummus on each tortilla, then add the curried tofu and vegetables of your choice.

Roll the tortillas to form wraps.

Nutritional Plan (per serving):

Cal: about 450 Cal.

Fat: 23g (about 46% of total Cal.)

PROT: 20g (about 18% of total Cal.)

Carbs: 46g (about 36% of total Cal.)

Fiber: 9g (about 32% of total Cal.)

Salmon Salad with Avocado and Spinach

Ingredients (for 2 servings):

8 oz salmon fillet (2 fillets of 4 oz each)

4 oz of fresh spinach

4 oz avocado, thinly sliced

2 oz cucumbers, cut into thin rounds

2 oz cherry tomatoes, cut in half

Olive oil extra virgin, 2 tablespoons

1 tbsp of lemon juice, fresh

1 tsp of maple syrup or honey (optional)

To taste, add salt and freshly ground black pepper.

For garnish, use fresh herbs (such as parsley or basil) (optional)

Preparation:

Preheat a grill or a skillet that doesn't stick to medium-high heat.

After giving the salmon fillets a quick coating with olive oil, season them with salt and pepper before placing them in the oven.

The salmon should be cooked through and have a light golden crust after 3 to 4 minutes on each side, depending on whether you're using a grill or a skillet.

Depending on the thickness of the fillets, cooking times may change.

In a large bowl, create a bed of fresh spinach.

Arrange the avocado slices, cucumber slices, and cherry tomatoes on top of the spinach.

Once cooked, cut the salmon into smaller pieces and lay them on the salad.

Olive oil, lemon juice, and honey should be mixed together in a small basin (if you want a touch of sweetness). A few drops of this vinaigrette should be added to the salad.

If you choose, top the dish with some freshly chopped herbs, and then season it with salt and pepper to taste.

As soon as possible, serve the Salmon Salad with Avocado and Spinach as a main dish because it is light and healthy.

Nutrition Plan (per serving, excluding salt and pepper):

Cal: about 400 Cal.

Fat: 27g (about 62% of total Cal.)

PROT: 26g (about 24% of total Cal.)

Carbs: 20g (about 14% of total Cal.)

Fiber: 10g

Tuna and Bean Salad

Servings: 2
Ingredients

6 oz canned tuna, drained

8 oz canned canned cannellini beans, rinsed and drained

Cherry tomatoes, sliced in half, 4 ounces

2 tsp of finely chopped red onion

2 tsp chopped fresh parsley

Lemon juice from one

Olive oil extra virgin, 2 tablespoons

To taste, add salt and pepper.

Preparation:

A large bowl should be used to combine tuna that has been drained, cannellini beans, cherry tomatoes that have been cut in half, red onion that has been diced, and fresh parsley that has been chopped.

In a small bowl, whisk together the lemon juice, olive oil, salt, and pepper to form a vinaigrette.

To ensure that all of the components of the tuna and bean salad receive a uniform coating, simply sprinkle the vinaigrette over the salad.

A tuna and bean salad can either be a main meal or a side dish, depending on how it is prepared.

Nutritional Plan (per serving):

Cal: about 380 Cal.

Fat: 16g (around 38% of the total Cal.)

PROT: 30g (around 32% of the total Cal.)

Carbs: 35g (around 30% of the total Cal.)

Fiber: 9g (about 24% of total Cal.)

Quinoa and Chickpea Salad with Roasted Vegetables

Ingredients (for 2 servings):

4 oz of raw quinoa

8 oz cooked chickpeas (rinsed and drained)

6 oz cherry tomatoes cut in half

4 oz zucchini, thinly sliced

4 oz. of thinly sliced red peppers

2 oz of thinly sliced red onion

Olive oil extra virgin, 2 tablespoons

Oregano, dry, 1 teaspoon

To taste, add salt and freshly ground black pepper.

2 tsp chopped fresh basil

Lemon juice from one

Preparation:

Set the oven's temperature to 200 °C, or 390 °F.

In a pot, cook the quinoa according to the instructions on the label. Typically, for 4 oz of raw quinoa, you will need 1 1/2 C of water. Cook the quinoa until it has absorbed all the water and is soft.

Prepare the roasted vegetables while the quinoa is heating up. On a baking sheet, arrange the onion slices, red bell pepper strips, and zucchini slices. Include some dried oregano a tablespoon of extra virgin olive oil, and season with salt and pepper to taste. After thorough mixing, the veggies should be baked for around twenty minutes or until they are tender and just beginning to brown.

All of the cooked ingredients, including quinoa, chickpeas, cherry tomatoes, roasted vegetables, and fresh basil, are mixed together in a large bowl.

In a low-sided dish, mix together one tablespoon of extra virgin olive oil and one tablespoon of lemon juice. To ensure that the dressing is distributed evenly, sprinkle this vinaigrette over the salad and then mix it thoroughly with your hands.

A quinoa and chickpea salad can either be a main dish or a side dish, depending on how it is prepared.

Nutrition Plan (per serving, excluding salt and pepper):

Cal: about 450 Cal.

Fat: 15g (around 30% of the total Cal.)

PROT: 15g (around 15% of the total Cal.)

Carbs: 65g (around 55% of the total Cal.)

Fiber: 12g (about 32% of total Cal.)

....

Zucchini Spaghetti with Avocado Pesto

Servings: 2
Ingredients

8 oz zucchini, cut into noodles

1 ripe avocado

2 tbsp of chopped, toasted walnuts

1 minced garlic clove

Lemon juice from one

Olive oil extra virgin, 2 tablespoons

To taste, add salt and pepper.

Preparation:

Use a spiralizer to create zucchini noodles or cut zucchini into julienne strips.

The ingredients for avocado pesto are as follows: avocado, pecans, lemon juice, olive oil, fresh basil, garlic that has been minced, and the seasonings salt and pepper.

Stir the zucchini noodles with the avocado pesto until well coated.

Serve zucchini noodles with avocado pesto as a main meal.

Curried Tofu with Broccoli and Spinach

Ingredients: Servings: 4

14 oz extra-strong tofu, cut into cubes

1 tbsp olive oil (0.5 oz)

1 red onion, thinly sliced

2 C fresh broccoli, cut into pieces (4 oz)

4 C fresh spinach (4 oz)

Light coconut milk, 1 can (13.5 oz)

2 tbsp of red curry paste (2 oz)

1 tbsp soy sauce (0.5 oz)

1 lime's juice

To taste, add salt and black pepper.

14 C chopped fresh cilantro (0.5 oz)

Preparation:

It is best to warm the olive oil in a large skillet at a medium heat setting of medium. Tofu that has been cut into cubes should be added and then cooked until it is golden brown all over. Place the

Nutritional Plan (per serving):

Cal: about 350 Cal.

Fat: 30g (around 77% of the total Cal.)

PROT: 6g (around 7% of the total Cal.)

Carbs: 20g (around 16% of the total Cal.)

Fiber: 8g (about 27% of total Cal.)

tofu on a dish and set it aside for later use.

The same skillet should then have onion slices added to it and cooked for about five minutes or until the slices are tender and have a light browning.

After five more minutes of heating in the pan, the broccoli should be crisp on the outside and tender on the inside.

After reducing the heat, stir in the red curry paste, coconut milk, soy sauce, and lime juice. Mix everything together in a large mixing bowl until it is well mixed.

Stir gently to coat the tofu with the curry sauce after adding it to the pan. Give it another two to three minutes to cook.

Stir in the fresh spinach until just wilted.

You should try the cuisine and then season it with salt and black pepper according to your preferences.

Warm up the broccoli, spinach, and curried tofu before serving, then top each portion with chopped fresh cilantro.

Nutritional Plan (per serving):

Cal: about 350 Cal.

Fat: 20g (about 51% of total Cal.)

PROT: 16g (about 18% of total Cal.)

Carbs: 32g (about 31% of total Cal.)

Fiber: 8g

....

Turmeric Chicken with Broccoli

Servings: 2
Ingredients

12 oz of cut-up chicken breast

8 oz broccoli, divided into florets

Olive oil extra virgin, 2 tablespoons

one tsp of turmeric powder

Paprika, half a teaspoon

To taste, add salt and pepper.

1 clove of garlic, minced

The juice of 1 lemon

2 tsp chopped fresh parsley

Preparation:
Combine the chicken pieces with the salt, pepper, paprika, and turmeric powder in a bowl.

In a frying pan, the olive oil needs to be heated over medium-high heat.

Add the marinated chicken and simmer for a further 5-7 minutes once the chicken is fully cooked and golden brown. Place the reserved chicken in a basin.

Cut up broccoli florets and minced garlic should be added to the same pan. The broccoli should be crisp and tender after 5 minutes of cooking.

Re-add the chicken to the pan and stir thoroughly.

Sprinkle chopped fresh parsley over the chicken and broccoli after squeezing lemon juice over them.

As a main course, serve broccoli and chicken with turmeric.

Nutritional Plan (per serving):

Cal: about 350 Cal.

Fat: 15g (about 39% of total Cal.)

PROT: 35g (about 38% of total Cal.)

Carbs: 21g (about 23% of total Cal.)

Fiber: 6g (about 16% of total Cal.)15.

....

Grilled Chicken Salad with Quinoa and Avocado

Servings: 2
Ingredients

8 oz grilled chicken breast, thinly sliced

4 oz of cooked quinoa

1 ripe avocado, cut into cubes

4 oz cherry tomatoes, cut in half

2 tbsp of toasted sunflower seeds

Olive oil extra virgin, 2 tablespoons

Lemon juice from one

To taste, add salt and pepper.

Preparation:

In a large bowl, combine thinly sliced grilled chicken breast, cooked quinoa, diced avocado, and halved cherry tomatoes.

Combine olive oil, lemon juice, salt, and pepper in a small bowl to make a vinaigrette.

After adding the vinaigrette, gently toss the salad.

Sprinkle the surface of the salad with toasted sunflower seeds.

Serve grilled chicken salad with quinoa and avocado as a main meal.

Nutritional Plan (per serving):
Cal: about 520 Cal.

Fat: 29g (about 50% of total Cal.)

PROT: 36g (about 28% of total Cal.)

Carbs: 35g (about 27% of total Cal.)

Fiber: 11g (about 32% of total Cal.)

Turkey Wraps with Grilled Vegetables

Servings: 2
Ingredients

8 oz thinly sliced turkey breast

4 whole wheat tortillas

4 oz grilled red peppers, cut into strips

4 oz. grilled zucchini, cut into strips

2 tbsp hummus

leaves of lettuce, to taste

To taste, add salt and pepper.

Preparation:

Spread some hummus on each whole-wheat tortilla.

Add sliced turkey breast, grilled red bell pepper strips, and grilled zucchini strips.

Salt and pepper the lettuce leaves to taste before adding them.

To make wraps, roll the tortillas.

As a main course, serve turkey wraps with grilled vegetables.

Nutritional Plan (per serving):

Cal: about 380 Cal.

Fat: 14g (about 33% of total Cal.)

PROT: 24g (about 26% of total Cal.)

Carbs: 47g (about 41% of total Cal.)

Fiber: 8g (about 20% of total Cal.)

....

Chickpea and Tomato Salad

Servings: 2
Ingredients

8 oz cooked chickpeas (rinsed and drained)

8 oz cherry tomatoes, cut in half

2 tsp of finely chopped red onion

Extra virgin olive oil and 2 tsp of chopped fresh parsley

Lemon juice from one

To taste, add salt and pepper.

Preparation:

In a large bowl, add the cooked chickpeas, diced cherry tomatoes, red onion, and fresh parsley.

Combine olive oil, lemon juice, salt, and pepper in a small bowl to make a vinaigrette.

After adding the vinaigrette, gently toss the salad.

Serve chickpea and tomato salad as a main meal or side dish.

Nutritional Plan (per serving):

Cal: about 320 Cal.

Fat: 15g (about 42% of total Cal.)

PROT: 10g (about 12% of total Cal.)

Carbs: 40g (about 46% of total Cal.)

Fiber: 9g (about 32% of total Cal.)

....

Spinach and Feta Quiche

Servings: 2
Ingredients
8 oz of fresh spinach

4 oz of crumbled feta cheese

4 eggs

Milk, one-fourth cup

1/4 C coarsely chopped red onion

To taste, add salt and pepper.

Extra virgin olive oil, 1 tablespoon

Preparation:

350°F (180°C) should be the oven's temperature.

Fresh spinach and crumbled feta are put in a bowl.

In a separate bowl, whisk the milk and eggs together.

Finely sliced red onion is combined with salt and pepper to taste.

An oven-safe dish should be greased with extra virgin olive oil.

The baking dish should be filled with the spinach and feta mixture.

Over the spinach and feta, drizzle the egg mixture.

For 30-35 minutes, or until golden brown and set in the center, bake quiche in a preheated oven.

Let cool slightly before cutting and serving.

Nutritional Plan (per serving):

Cal: about 320 Cal.

Fat: 20g (about 56% of total Cal.)

PROT: 16g (about 20% of total Cal.)

Carbs: 18g (about 24% of total Cal.)

Fiber: 4g (about 14% of total Cal.)

Salmon and Potato Salad

Servings: 2
Ingredients

8 oz cooked salmon, crumbled

8 oz red potatoes, boiled and diced

4 oz cucumbers, diced

2 tsp of finely chopped red onion

2 tbsp light mayonnaise

2 tbsp of Greek yogurt

The juice of 1 lemon

1 tbsp finely chopped fresh parsley Salt and pepper as desired.

Preparation:

Combine cooked salmon crumbles in a large bowl, boiled and diced red potatoes, diced cucumbers, finely chopped red onion, light mayonnaise, and Greek yogurt.

Add lemon juice and chopped fresh parsley.

Mix all ingredients gently until thoroughly blended.

Serve potato salad and salmon as a main course or side dish.

Nutritional Plan (per serving):
Cal: about 420 Cal.

Fat: 18g (about 38% of total Cal.)

PROT: 23g (about 22% of total Cal.)

Carbs: 42g (about 40% of total Cal.)

Fiber: 5g (about 18% of total Cal.)

Chicken Salad with Avocado and Quinoa

Servings: 2
Ingredients

8 oz grilled chicken breast, thinly sliced

4 oz of cooked quinoa

1 ripe avocado, cut into cubes

4 oz cucumbers, diced

4 oz cherry tomatoes, cut in half

2 tbsp of toasted sunflower seeds

Olive oil extra virgin, 2 tablespoons

Lemon juice from one

To taste, add salt and pepper.

Preparation:

In a large bowl, combine thinly sliced grilled chicken breast, cooked quinoa, diced avocado, diced cucumbers, and halved cherry tomatoes.

Combine olive oil, lemon juice, salt, and pepper in a small bowl to make a vinaigrette.

After adding the vinaigrette, gently toss the salad.

Sprinkle the surface of the salad with toasted sunflower seeds.

Serve chicken salad with avocado and quinoa as a main meal.

Nutritional Plan (per serving):
Cal: about 520 Cal.

Fat: 29g (about 50% of total Cal.)

PROT: 36g (about 28% of total Cal.)

Carbs: 35g (about 27% of total Cal.)

Fiber: 11g (about 32% of total Cal.)

Grilled Salmon with Dill and Lemon Sauce

Ingredients (for 2 servings):

12 oz of salmon fillets (about 2 fillets of 6 oz each)

Extra virgin olive oil, 1 ounce

Fresh lemon juice, 1 ounce

1 tsp grated lemon peel and

1 tbsp freshly chopped dill

To taste, add salt and freshly ground black pepper.

Preparation:

Set the grill's temperature to medium-high.

In a small bowl, mix the grated lemon zest, lemon juice, chopped fresh dill, and olive oil. Add salt and pepper to taste.

Apply a little coating of the dill and lemon sauce to both sides of the salmon fillets.

The salmon fillets should be placed on the heating grill. The salmon should be cooked and have excellent grill marks after 3 to 4 minutes on each side of the pan.

Place the grilled salmon fillets on a

serving plate and, if you like, top with additional fresh dill and lemon slices.

Serve grilled salmon with dill and lemon sauce hot.

Nutrition Plan (per serving, excluding salt and pepper):

Cal: about 315 Cal.

Fat: 21g (about 60% of total Cal.)

PROT: 31g (about 39% of total Cal.)

Carbs: 2g (about 1% of total Cal.)

Fiber: 0g

Chickpea and Beet Salad with Cumin Hummus

Ingredients (for 2 servings):

4 oz of cooked chickpeas (about 1/2 cup)

4 oz of cooked beets (about 1/2 cup)

2 tbsp cumin hummus

2 tbsp of lemon juice

Extra virgin olive oil, 1 tablespoon

one-half tsp of cumin powder

To taste, add salt and freshly ground black pepper.

A total of 2 C of mixed lettuce (or your favorite variety)

1/4 C finely chopped, toasted walnuts

1/4 C of feta cheese crumbles

garnishing with fresh parsley (optional)

Preparation:

Cooked beets and cooked chickpeas should be combined in a big bowl.

In a small bowl, combine the cumin humus, lemon juice, olive oil, cumin powder, salt, and pepper to make a vinaigrette.

The vinaigrette should be equally distributed throughout the chickpea and beet salad after being added.

Add mixed leaf lettuce leaves and mix again to combine all ingredients.

Place the salad on two plates for serving.

Sprinkle the toasted walnuts and crumbled feta cheese over the salad.

If desired, garnish with fresh parsley.

As a side dish or a light main entrée, serve the salad.

Nutritional Plan (per serving):
Cal: about 350 Cal.

Fat: 20g (about 51% of total Cal.)

PROT: 12g (about 14% of total Cal.)

Carbs: 32g (about 35% of total Cal.)

Fiber: 8g (about 22% of total Cal.)

Quinoa Salad with Chickpeas and Avocado

Ingredients (for 2 servings):

4 oz of raw quinoa

8 oz cooked chickpeas (rinsed and drained)

4 oz avocado, diced

2 oz cucumber, diced

2 oz cherry tomatoes, cut in half

2 oz of finely chopped red onion (optional)

Olive oil extra virgin, 2 tablespoons

One lime's juice

Add salt and freshly ground black pepper to taste.

For garnish, use fresh parsley or cilantro leaves (optional)

Preparation:

The raw quinoa should be well rinsed under cold running water before cooking, as directed on the package. Typically, for 4 oz of quinoa, you will need 1 C of water. Once cooked, let it cool.

Combine the cooked quinoa, cooked chickpeas, diced avocado, cucumber, and cherry tomatoes in a sizable bowl...

If you want a touch of spiciness, you can also add finely chopped red onion.

Olive oil, lime juice, salt, and pepper are all ingredients in a vinaigrette.

To uniformly distribute the vinaigrette, drizzle it over the salad and gently mix.

If preferred, garnish with fresh parsley or cilantro.

Serve Quinoa Salad with Chickpeas and Avocado as a main meal or side dish.

Nutrition Plan (per serving, excluding salt and pepper):

Cal: about 450 Cal.

Fat: 21g (about 42% of total Cal.)

PROT: 12g (about 11% of total Cal.)

Carbs: 55g (about 47% of total Cal.)

Fiber: 12g (about 32% of total Cal.)

Grilled Salmon with Ginger and Lemon Sauce

Ingredients (for 2 servings):

2 salmon fillets, 6 oz each

Olive oil, 2 tablespoons

1/4 C freshly grated ginger

1 lemon's juice and zest

2 garlic cloves, minced finely

Honey, one teaspoon

To taste, add salt and freshly ground black pepper.

Fresh parsley for garnish (optional)

Preparation:

Heat the grill or barbecue to a moderately hot setting.

Combine the olive oil, honey, minced garlic, lemon juice, lemon zest, ginger, salt, and pepper in a small bowl to make the marinade.

On both sides of the salmon fillets, liberally brush on the marinade.

The salmon fillets need to be fried for three to four minutes on each side or until they are fully cooked and have a thin golden crust. Depending on the thickness of the salmon, the cooking time will vary, so make sure it is done.

During the last few minutes of cooking, you can further brush the salmon with some of the remaining marinade to intensify the flavor.

Transfer the cooked salmon to a serving tray once it is done.

If preferred, top with freshly chopped parsley while serving.

Nutritional Plan (per serving):

Cal: about 350 Cal.

Fat: 20g (about 51% of total Cal.)

PROT: 34g (about 36% of total Cal.)

Carbs: 9g (about 13% of total Cal.)

Fiber: 1g (about 4% of total Cal.)

....

Curried Tofu with Grilled Vegetables

Ingredients (for 2 servings):

8 oz of tofu (about half a package)

4 oz eggplant (about 1/2 eggplant)

4 oz zucchini (about 1 small zucchini)

4 oz of mixed peppers (about 1 bell pepper)

2 oz red onion (about 1/2 onion)

Extra virgin olive oil, 1 tablespoon

2 tbsp of red curry paste

1 C of coconut milk (8 oz)

1 tbsp of soy sauce

1/9 C brown sugar

To taste, add salt and freshly ground black pepper.

Lime or lemon juice for garnish

Fresh basil leaves for garnish

Preparation:

Tofu should be cut into roughly 1-inch chunks.

Make bite-sized cuts with the peppers, zucchini, and eggplant. The red onion should be thinly cut.

Tofu should be thoroughly coated after being combined with red curry paste in a big dish.

Olive oil should be heated over medium-high heat in a nonstick skillet. Cook the tofu that has been marinated in the mixture until crisp and golden. Tofu should be taken out of the pan and placed aside.

Include the chopped vegetables in the same pan. They should be cooked for a few minutes until crisp but still soft.

Reintroduce the tofu to the pan along with the vegetables.

Over the tofu and vegetable combination, pour the coconut milk. Salt, pepper, brown sugar, and soy sauce should be added. Cook for another 2 to 3 minutes after thoroughly stirring.

Serve curried tofu with barbecued vegetables hot, garnished with fresh lime or lemon juice and basil leaves.

Nutrition Plan (per serving, excluding lime or lemon juice and basil leaves):

Cal: about 380 Cal.

Fat: 29g (about 68% of total Cal.)

PROT: 11g (about 12% of total Cal.)

Carbs: 26g (about 20% of total Cal.)

Fiber: 7g (about 25% of total Cal.)

Grilled Salmon with Lemon and Avocado Sauce

Ingredients (for 2 servings):

2 fillets of salmon (about 6 oz each)

1 mature avocado (about 6 oz)

Olive oil extra virgin, 2 tablespoons

Lemon juice from one

lemon zest, grated

2 tsp freshly chopped parsley

Add salt and freshly ground black pepper to taste.

Preparation:

Set the grill's temperature to medium-high.

In a separate bowl, make the lemon-avocado salsa. Mash the avocado in a bowl and season with salt and pepper to taste. Add the lemon juice, zest, and 1 tablespoon of olive oil. Until the mixture becomes creamy, stir constantly.

The salmon fillets should be lightly coated in 1 tablespoon of olive oil and taste-tested with salt and black pepper.

The salmon fillets should be cooked through and flake readily with a fork after 4 to 5 minutes of cooking per side on a hot grill.

Grilled salmon should be topped with a lot of the lemon avocado sauce.

If desired, decorate with lemon slices or extra parsley leaves.

Nutrition Plan (per serving, excluding salt and pepper):

Cal: about 400 Cal.

Fat: 28g (about 63% of total Cal.)

PROT: 34g (about 34% of total Cal.)

Carbs: 14g (about 13% of total Cal.)

Fiber: 9g (about 36% of total Cal.)

....

Quinoa with Curried Vegetables

Ingredients (for 2 servings):

4 oz of quinoa

8 oz of vegetable broth

4 oz zucchini, diced

4 oz of red bell pepper, thinly sliced

4 oz of carrots, thinly sliced

Green peas, 4 oz.

Olive oil, 2 tablespoons

Red curry paste, one tablespoon

One-half tsp of turmeric powder

To taste, add salt and freshly ground black pepper.

Freshly cut parsley (optional, for garnish)

Preparation:

In a colander, thoroughly rinse the quinoa

under running water until the water is clear.

In a pot, bring vegetable broth to a boil. Before adding the rinsed quinoa, reduce the heat. The quinoa should be cooked for a further 15 to 20 minutes, or until it has absorbed all the liquid and turned translucent, under cover. Set aside.

In a large skillet set over medium heat, olive oil should be heated. After adding the carrots, cook them for around 3–4 minutes.

Add the zucchini, peppers, and peas. The vegetables should be crisp and delicate after an additional 3–4 minutes of cooking.

Turmeric and red curry paste should be added to the vegetables. Stir the curry thoroughly to spread it evenly.

Stir the vegetables and cooked quinoa together until everything is evenly distributed. After tasting, season with salt and pepper to taste.

Quinoa with Curried Vegetables should be served hot, with optional fresh parsley garnish.

Nutrition Plan (per serving, excluding salt and pepper):

Cal: about 350 Cal.

Fat: 11g (about 28% of total Cal.)

PROT: 10g (about 11% of total Cal.)

Carbs: 52g (about 61% of total Cal.)

Sugars: 7g

Fiber: 9g

....

Beet Salad with Spinach and Walnuts

Ingredients (for 2 servings):

8 oz of cooked beets (about 1 cup)

4 oz of fresh spinach (about 4 cups)

2 oz roasted walnuts (about 1/2 cup)

Olive oil extra virgin, 2 tablespoons

1/fourth C balsamic vinegar

1 tsp of maple syrup or honey

To taste, add salt and freshly ground black pepper.

2 oz goat cheese (optional)

Toasted sesame seeds for garnish (optional)

Preparation:

Start by peeling the cooked beets and cutting them into thin slices.

Beets and fresh spinach, both cut, should be combined in a big basin.

Combine the olive oil, balsamic vinegar, honey (or maple syrup), salt, and pepper in a small bowl to make a vinaigrette.

To uniformly spread the vinaigrette, drizzle it over the beet and spinach salad and gently mix.

Add the toasted walnuts to the salad and mix again.

If you wish, you can crumble goat cheese over the salad and sprinkle some toasted sesame seeds for an extra garnish.

Serve beet salad with spinach as a side dish or a light main course.

Nutrition Plan (per serving, excluding goat cheese and sesame seeds):

Cal: about 250 Cal.

Fat: 20g (about 69% of total Cal.)

PROT: 4g (about 7% of total Cal.)

Carbs: 15g (about 24% of total Cal.)

Fiber: 4g (about 16% of total Cal.)

Spring Quinoa with Roasted Vegetables and Tomato Sauce

Ingredients (for 2 servings):

4 oz of quinoa (about 1/2 cup)

8 oz of cherry tomatoes (about 1 cup)

4 oz of zucchini (about 1/2 cup)

4 oz eggplant (about 1/2 cup)

4 oz of red bell bell pepper (about 1/2 cup)

Olive oil, 2 tablespoons

2 garlic cloves, minced finely

Oregano, dry, 1 teaspoon

To taste, add salt and freshly ground black pepper.

4 oz of tomato sauce (about 1/2 cup)

Fresh basil for garnish

Preparation:

400 °F or 200 °C for the oven setting.

Slice the zucchini, eggplant, and red bell pepper into dice. Moreover, divide the cherry tomatoes in half.

Put cut vegetables in a line on a baking sheet. Add salt, pepper, olive oil, minced garlic, and dried oregano to season. To ensure that the vegetables are well-seasoned, stir thoroughly.

For 20 to 25 minutes, or until they are soft and have a light browning, the vegetables should be cooked in the preheated oven. During cooking, stir the vegetables once or twice.

Following a thorough rinse under cold running water, quinoa should be cooked according to the package's instructions.

When the vegetables are cooked through, take the pan out of the oven and leave it aside.

Over medium heat, warm the tomato sauce in a frying pan.

Mix thoroughly after adding the roasted veggies to the tomato sauce.

On two plates, place the cooked quinoa and top with the roasted veggie sauce.

Serve hot with fresh basil as a garnish.

Nutritional Plan (per serving):

Cal: about 400 Cal.

Fat: 14g (about 31% of total Cal.)

PROT: 10g (about 10% of total Cal.)

Carbs: 63g (about 59% of total Cal.)

Fiber: 9g (about 24% of total Cal.)

....

Spring Quinoa with Grilled Vegetables and Lemon Sauce

Ingredients (for 2 servings):

4 oz of raw quinoa

8 oz asparagus, chopped

6 oz zucchini, cut into thin rounds

Cherry tomatoes, sliced in half, 4 ounces

Feta cheese, crumbled, 2 ounces

Olive oil extra virgin, 2 tablespoons

Lemon juice from one

1 tsp of lemon peel, shredded

Add salt and freshly ground black pepper to taste.

2 tablespoons freshly minced parsley

Preparation:

Thoroughly rinse the quinoa in cool, running water. Place aside.

Heat a nonstick skillet or grill to medium-high.

In a bowl, combine the zucchini and asparagus with 1 tablespoon of olive oil. Grill the mixture for 3 to 4 minutes or until it is soft and lightly browned. During the last two minutes of cooking, add the cherry tomatoes. Vegetables should be taken from the grill and put aside.

Bring to a boil in a saucepan 1.5 times as much water as quinoa. Turn the heat down to medium-low after adding the quinoa. Quinoa needs around 15 minutes of cooking time under cover to finish cooking and absorb all the liquid. Remove from heat, then stand aside for five minutes. After that, shell the quinoa with a fork.

To prepare the lemon sauce, combine the lemon juice, grated lemon zest, one table spoon of olive oil, and salt and black pepper to taste in a mixing bowl.

Mix the cooked quinoa, the veggies that have been grilled, the crumbled feta cheese, and the lemon sauce together in a big bowl. Combine each component of the dish thoroughly.

Garnish with fresh chopped parsley before serving.

Nutrition Plan (per serving, excluding salt and pepper):

Cal: about 400 Cal.

Fat: 20g (about 45% of total Cal.)

PROT: 14g (about 14% of total Cal.)

Carbs: 47g (about 41% of total Cal.)

Fiber: 8g (about 32% of total Cal.)

Honey Mustard Salmon Salad

Servings: 2
Ingredients

8 oz salmon fillet, cooked and crumbled

4 oz of fresh spinach

1/2 apple, diced

2 tbsp chopped, toasted pecans

2 tsp of finely chopped red onion

Olive oil extra virgin, 2 tablespoons

Honey, 1 tablespoon

1 tbsp Dijon mustard

Lemon juice from one

To taste, add salt and pepper.

Preparation:

In a sizable bowl, the following ingredients should be mixed together: cooked and crumbled salmon, fresh spinach, apple slices, toasted pecans that have been diced, and finely chopped red onion.

Vinaigrette can be prepared by whisking together in a small bowl extra virgin olive oil, honey, Dijon mustard, lemon juice, and seasonings such as salt and pepper.

After adding the vinaigrette, gently toss the salad.

As a main course, offer the honey-mustard salmon salad.

Nutritional Plan (per serving):

Cal: about 400 Cal.

Fat: 24g (about 54% of total Cal.)

PROT: 27g (about 26% of total Cal.)

....

Chicken Curry Wraps with Chickpeas

Servings: 2
Ingredients

8 oz chicken breast, diced

cooked chickpeas, 4 oz (rinsed and drained)

2 tortillas made of whole wheat

1/2 avocado, thinly sliced

2 tbsp of Greek yogurt

2 tsp curry powder

1 tbsp extra virgin olive oil

To taste, add salt and pepper.

Preparation:

It is best to bring the olive oil to temperature in a frying pan set over medium-high heat.

Cook the chicken breast in the form of dice until the chicken is golden and has been cooked through.

Carbs: 28g (about 20% of total Cal.)

Fiber: 5g (about 15% of total Cal.)

The curry powder and chickpeas that have been cooked should both be added to the pan containing the chicken. After fully stirring the pot, continue cooking for another two to three minutes.

In a modest bowl, salt and pepper should be mixed with Greek yogurt according to personal preference.

Spread some Greek yogurt on each whole-wheat tortilla.

Add the curry chicken and chickpeas to the tortilla, then lay thin slices of avocado on top.

Roll up the tortilla to form the wrap.

Serve chicken curry wraps with chickpeas as a meal.

Nutritional Plan (per serving):

Cal: about 420 Cal.

Fat: 17g (about 36% of total Cal.)

PROT: 30g (about 29% of total Cal.)

Carbs: 40g (about 35% of total Cal.)

Fiber: 8g (about 22% of total Cal.)

....

Grilled Salmon with Yogurt and Lemon Sauce

Servings: 2
Ingredients

2 fillets of salmon (roughly 6 oz each)

Greek yoghurt, 4 ounces

Lemon juice from one

2 tablespoons of finely chopped fresh parsley and 2 tablespoons of finely chopped fresh chives

Salt and pepper should be added to taste.

Preparation:
Set the grill's temperature to medium-high.

To make the sauce, combine Greek yogurt, lemon juice, fresh parsley that has been chopped, chives, salt, and pepper in a bowl.

The salmon fillets should be grilled on the grill for three to four minutes on each side.

Serve the grilled salmon with the yogurt and lemon sauce as a topping.

Nutritional Plan (per serving):

Cal: about 350 Cal.

Fat: 18g (about 46% of total Cal.)

PROT: 35g (about 39% of total Cal.)

Carbs: 12g (about 14% of total Cal.)

Fiber: 1g (about 3% of total Cal.)

....

Curried Chickpea Salad

Servings: 2
Ingredients

8 oz cooked chickpeas (rinsed and drained)

1/2 cucumber, diced

1 tomato, diced

2 tsp of finely chopped red onion

Olive oil extra virgin, 2 tablespoons

curry powder, 1 teaspoon

a half-teaspoon of sweet paprika

To taste, add salt and pepper.

Fresh coriander leaves for garnish.

Preparation:

The cooked chickpeas, sliced cucumber, diced tomato, and finely chopped red onion should all be combined in a big bowl.

To prepare a vinaigrette, take a small bowl and mix together some extra virgin olive oil, curry powder, and sweet paprika, along with some salt and pepper.

The chickpea salad will benefit from the addition of the vinaigrette, which should be fully mixed in.

Garnish with fresh cilantro leaves.

Serve curried chickpea salad as a meal or side dish.

Nutritional Plan (per serving):

Cal: about 320 Cal.

Fat: 15g (about 42% of total Cal.)

PROT: 11g (about 14% of total Cal.)

Carbs: 38g (about 44% of total Cal.)

Fiber: 8g (about 23% of total Cal.)

....

Spinach Salad with Grilled Salmon and Avocado

Servings: 2
Ingredients

8 oz of grilled salmon fillet

4 oz of fresh spinach

1 avocado, sliced

1/4 C chopped, toasted pecans

Feta cheese, crumbled, 2 tsp (optional)

Olive oil extra virgin, 2 tablespoons

Lemon juice from one

To taste, add salt and pepper.

Preparation:

Grill the salmon fillet until it is cooked through.

Combine fresh spinach, avocado slices, roasted and chopped nuts, and feta cheese crumbles in a sizable bowl (if desired).

Vinaigrette can be made by combining extra virgin olive oil, lemon juice, salt, and pepper in a small bowl. This will create the dressing.

After the vinaigrette has been added, give the salad a light tossing.

Cut the grilled salmon into pieces and lay them on the salad.

Serve spinach salad with grilled salmon and avocado as a main meal.

Nutritional Plan (per serving):

Cal: about 450 Cal.

Fat: 33g (about 66% of total Cal.)

PROT: 25g (about 22% of total Cal.)

Carbs: 22g (about 20% of total Cal.)

Fiber: 10g (about 29% of total Cal.)

....

Chicken Curry with Coconut and Quinoa

Servings: 2
Ingredients

8 oz chicken breast, diced

4 oz of cooked quinoa

Coconut milk, 4 ounces

Red curry paste, one tablespoon

Extra virgin olive oil, half a tablespoon

1/2 onion, chopped finely

a single minced garlic clove

Freshly grated ginger, half a teaspoon

One-half tsp of turmeric powder

To taste, add salt and pepper.

Garnish with fresh cilantro (optional)

Preparation:

It is best to bring the olive oil to temperature in a frying pan set over medium-high heat.

Add ginger that has been grated, garlic that has been finely minced, and onion that has been cut very finely. Cook until the food is fragrant and has a golden color.

Cook till golden brown after adding the cubed chicken breast.

To flavor the chicken, combine the red curry paste and the turmeric powder.

After adding the coconut milk, bring the pan to a boil by bringing it to a boil.

After the chicken is cooked through and the sauce has become somewhat more viscous, turn the heat down to low and continue to simmer for five to seven minutes.

Over cooked quinoa, serve the chicken curry with coconut.

Fresh cilantro as a garnish (if desired).

Nutritional Plan (per serving):

Cal: about 450 Cal.

Fat: 20g (about 40% of total Cal.)

PROT: 28g (about 26% of total Cal.)

Carbs: 42g (about 34% of total Cal.)

Fiber: 6g (about 17% of total Cal.)

....

Honey Mustard Chicken Salad

Servings: 2
Ingredients

8 oz chicken breast, cooked and cut into strips

4 oz of fresh spinach

1/2 apple, diced

2 tbsp pecans, toasted and chopped

2 tsp of finely chopped red onion

Olive oil extra virgin, 2 tablespoons

Honey, 1 tablespoon

1 tbsp Dijon mustard

Lemon juice from one

To taste, add salt and pepper.

Preparation:

Sliced cooked chicken breast, fresh spinach, sliced apple, chopped toasted pecans, and finely chopped red onion are all combined in a big bowl.

Vinaigrette can be prepared by whisking together in a small bowl extra virgin olive oil, honey, Dijon mustard, lemon juice, and seasonings such as salt and pepper.

After adding the vinaigrette, gently toss the salad.

Serve chicken salad with honey mustard as the main course.

Nutritional Plan (per serving):

Cal: about 420 Cal.

Fat: 22g (about 47% of total Cal.)

PROT: 28g (about 27% of total Cal.)

Carbs: 34g (about 26% of total Cal.)

Fiber: 6g (about 18% of total Cal.)

....

Chicken Curry with Mixed Vegetables and Brown Rice

Servings: 2
Ingredients

8 oz chicken breast, diced

4 oz cooked brown rice

4 oz of coconut milk

1 tbsp yellow curry paste

1/2 zucchini, cut into rounds

a half of a red bell pepper, thinly sliced.

A half of a carrot, thinly sliced.

1/2 an onion, cut finely.

1/2 of a finely chopped garlic clove.

Extra virgin olive oil, 1 tablespoon.

To taste, add salt and pepper.

Preparation:

It is best to bring the olive oil to temperature in a frying pan set over medium-high heat.

Add the minced onion as well as the garlic that has been minced. Cook until the food is fragrant and has a golden color.

Cook till golden brown after adding the cubed chicken breast.

To flavor the chicken, add the yellow curry paste and thoroughly combine.

Cook for an additional 3–4 minutes after adding the mixed veggies (zucchini, red bell pepper, and carrot).

After adding the coconut milk, bring the pan to a boil by bringing it to a boil.

Once the chicken is cooked through and the vegetables are tender, turn the heat down to medium and let the dish continue to boil for another five to seven minutes.

Serve chicken curry with mixed vegetables over cooked brown rice.

Nutritional Plan (per serving):

Cal: about 480 Cal.

Fat: 17g (about 32% of total Cal.)

PROT: 27g (about 22% of total Cal.)

Carbs: 58g (about 46% of total Cal.)

Fiber: 6g (about 17% of total Cal.)

....

Grilled Chicken with Avocado and Tomato Sauce

Servings: 2
Ingredients

8 oz of grilled chicken breast

1 avocado, sliced

1 tomato, diced

1/4 of a red onion, cut finely.

Olive oil extra virgin, 2 tablespoons.

One lime juice.

To taste, add salt and pepper.

Garnish with fresh cilantro (optional).

Preparation:

Grill the chicken breast until it is cooked through.

A large bowl should have pieces of avocado, tomatoes, and red onion that have been finely diced, all of which should be put together.

In a small bowl, combine the ingredients for a vinaigrette as follows: extra virgin olive oil, lime juice, salt, and pepper.

Then, gently combine the avocado and tomato salad with the vinaigrette.

Lay the chopped-up grilled chicken breast over the salad.

Fresh cilantro as a garnish (if desired).

Nutritional Plan (per serving):

Cal: about 450 Cal.

Fat: 29g (about 58% of total Cal.)

PROT: 32g (about 29% of total Cal.)

Carbs: 20g (about 13% of total Cal.)

Fiber: 9g (about 26% of total Cal.)

Curried Chickpea Salad with Grilled Chicken

Servings: 2
Ingredients

8 oz grilled chicken breast, cut into strips

4 oz cooked chickpeas (rinsed and drained)

4 C romaine lettuce, cut into strips

a half of a red bell pepper, thinly sliced.

1/4 of a thinly sliced red onion.

Olive oil extra virgin, 2 tablespoons.

1 tsp vinegar made from apple cider.

Curry powder, 1 teaspoon.

To taste, add salt and pepper.

Preparation:

Combine cooked chickpeas, romaine lettuce strips, thinly sliced red onion, and red bell pepper strips in a big bowl.

Vinaigrette can be made by combining extra virgin olive oil, apple cider vinegar, curry powder, salt, and pepper in a small bowl. This will produce the finished product.

Add the vinaigrette to the chickpea salad and thoroughly combine.

On top of the salad, arrange the grilled chicken breast slices.

Serve curried chickpea salad with grilled chicken as a main meal.

Nutritional Plan (per serving):
Cal: about 400 Cal.

Fat: 17g (about 38% of total Cal.)

PROT: 33g (about 33% of total Cal.)

Carbs: 32g (about 29% of total Cal.)

Fiber: 9g (about 26% of total Cal.)

Quinoa Bowl with Sesame Tofu

Servings: 2
Ingredients

8 oz tofu, diced and marinated in soy sauce and sesame oil

4 oz of cooked quinoa

2 C of steamed broccoli

1/2 avocado, sliced

2 tbsp of toasted sesame seeds

Soy sauce, two tablespoons.

Sesame seed oil, one tablespoon.

Rice vinegar, 1 tsp.

Freshly grated ginger, 1/2 tsp.

Minced garlic, 1/2 teaspoon.

To taste, add salt and pepper.

Preparation:

The marinated tofu should be crisp and golden brown after grilling.

Cooked quinoa, steamed broccoli, avocado slices, and toasted sesame seeds should all be combined in a big bowl.

In order to make a vinaigrette, mix the following ingredients together in a small bowl: soy sauce, sesame oil, rice vinegar, grated ginger, and chopped garlic.

Mix thoroughly after adding the vinaigrette to the quinoa bowl.

On top of the quinoa, arrange the cubes of sesame tofu.

Serve the quinoa bowl with sesame tofu as a meal.

Nutritional Plan (per serving):

Cal: about 440 Cal.

Fat: 24g (about 49% of total Cal.)

PROT: 21g (about 19% of total Cal.)

Carbs: 39g (about 32% of total Cal.)

Fiber: 9g (about 26% of total Cal.)

Curried Tofu with Quinoa and Vegetables

Servings: 2
Ingredients

8 oz tofu, cut into cubes

4 oz of cooked quinoa

4 oz broccoli, steamed

4 oz carrots, thinly sliced

4 oz cauliflower, steamed

4 oz. of finely sliced onion.

4 oz. of coarsely sliced garlic clove.

Olive oil extra virgin, 2 tablespoons.

Green curry paste, 2 tablespoons.

Light coconut milk, 1 cup.

To taste, add salt and pepper.

Garnish with fresh cilantro (optional).

Preparation:

It is best to bring the olive oil to temperature in a frying pan set over medium-high heat.

Add the minced onion as well as the garlic that has been minced. Cook until the food is fragrant and has a golden color.

After adding the tofu dice, continue to heat the mixture until it becomes golden brown on all sides.

To flavor the tofu, add the green curry paste and thoroughly combine.

Broccoli, carrots, and cauliflower should be added now and cooked for an additional 3 to 4 minutes.

After adding the coconut milk, bring the pan to a boil by bringing it to a boil.

Turn the heat down to low, cover the pot, and let it simmer for about five to seven minutes, or until the vegetables are tender and the tofu is completely covered with curry.

As a main dish, combine quinoa and curry tofu.

Fresh cilantro as a garnish (if desired).

Nutritional Plan (per serving):

Cal: about 480 Cal.

Fat: 29g (around 54% of the total Cal.)

PROT: 17g (around 15% of the total Cal.)

Carbs: 45g (around 31% of the total Cal.)

Fiber: 6g (about 21% of total Cal.)

....

Grilled Salmon and Avocado Salad

Servings: 2
Ingredients

8 oz of grilled salmon fillet

4 oz of fresh spinach

1 avocado, sliced

1/4 C chopped, toasted pecans.

Feta cheese, crumbled, 2 tsp (optional).

Olive oil extra virgin, 2 tablespoons.

One lemon juice.

To taste, add salt and pepper.

Preparation:

Grill the salmon fillet until it is cooked through.

Combine fresh spinach, avocado slices, roasted and chopped nuts, and feta cheese crumbles in a sizable bowl (if desired).

Vinaigrette can be made by combining extra virgin olive oil, lemon juice, salt, and pepper in a small bowl. This will create the dressing.

After the vinaigrette has been added, give the salad a light tossing.

Cut the grilled salmon into pieces and lay them on the salad.

Serve the grilled salmon and avocado salad as a main meal.

Nutritional Plan (per serving):

Cal: about 450 Cal.

Fat: 33g (about 66% of total Cal.)

PROT: 25g (about 22% of total Cal.)

Carbs: 22g (about 20% of total Cal.)

Fiber: 10g (about 29% of total Cal.)

Chicken Teriyaki Bowl with Vegetables

Servings: 2
Ingredients

8 oz chicken breast cut into strips

4 oz of steamed broccoli

4 oz carrots, thinly sliced

4 oz of red bell pepper, thinly sliced

4 oz of thinly sliced red onion

4 oz of cooked quinoa

2 tbsp teriyaki sauce

Extra virgin olive oil, 1 tablespoon

garnishing with sesame seeds (optional)

Preparation:

It is best to bring the olive oil to temperature in a frying pan set over medium-high heat.

Cook the chicken breast strips in a skillet, making sure to turn them occasionally until both sides are golden brown.

After adding the steamed vegetables, continue cooking for an additional three to four minutes (broccoli, carrots, red bell pepper, and red onion).

Mix thoroughly before adding the teriyaki sauce.

Place the cooked quinoa in bowls for dishing.

Pour the chicken and vegetable mix over the quinoa.

Garnish with sesame seeds (if desired).

Nutritional Plan (per serving):

Cal: about 400 Cal.

Fat: 12g (about 27% of total Cal.)

PROT: 32g (about 31% of total Cal.)

Carbs: 42g (about 42% of total Cal.)

Fiber: 8g (about 25% of total Cal.)

....

Pesto Quinoa Salad with Tomatoes and Black Beans

Servings: 2
Ingredients
8 oz of cooked quinoa

4 oz cherry tomatoes, cut in half

4 oz of cooked black beans (rinsed and drained)

fresh basil leaves weighing 2 ounces

2 oz of crumbled feta cheese (optional)

2 tbsp of pesto

One tablespoon of extra virgin olive oil

The lemon juice extracted from one

Salt and pepper should be added to taste.

Preparation:

In a sizable bowl, the following ingredients should be combined: cooked quinoa, cherry tomatoes cut in half, cooked black beans, and fresh basil leaves.

In order to make a vinaigrette, put the lemon juice, salt, and pepper in a small bowl along with the pesto, extra virgin olive oil, and lemon juice.

After adding the vinaigrette, gently toss the salad.

Add crumbled feta cheese (if desired).

Serve the pesto quinoa salad as a main meal or side dish.

Nutritional Plan (per serving):

Cal: about 430 Cal.

Fat: 14g (around 29% of the total Cal.)

PROT: 16g (around 15% of the total Cal.)

Carbs: 64g (around 56% of the total Cal.)

Fiber: 10g (about 33% of total Cal.)

....

Couscous Bowl with Grilled Chicken and Vegetables

Servings: 2
Ingredients

8 oz grilled chicken breast, cut into strips

4 oz of cooked couscous

4 oz eggplant, diced and grilled

4 oz zucchini, diced and grilled

4 oz dried tomatoes in oil, chopped

Two teaspoons of unrefined extra virgin olive oil.

Juice from half a lemon, one tablespoon.

One tbsp of dried oregano.

To taste, add salt and pepper.

Feta cheese in crumbles as a garnish (optional).

Preparation:

In a large bowl, combine cooked couscous, grilled eggplant, grilled zucchini, and chopped sun-dried tomatoes.

To prepare a vinaigrette, take a small bowl and mix together the extra virgin olive oil, lemon juice, dried oregano, and some salt and pepper.

Mix thoroughly after adding the vinaigrette to the bowl of couscous.

Over the couscous, arrange the chicken breast strips that have been grilled.

Add feta cheese crumbles as a garnish (if desired).

Nutritional Plan (per serving):

Cal: about 480 Cal.

Fat: 19g (about 35% of total Cal.)

PROT: 32g (about 27% of total Cal.)

Carbs: 46g (about 38% of total Cal.)

Fiber: 8g (about 25% of total Cal.)

Chili Chicken with Broccoli and Basmati Rice

Servings: 2
Ingredients

8 oz chicken breast cut into strips

4 oz of steamed broccoli

4 oz of cooked basmati rice

Chili sauce, two tablespoons.

Extra virgin olive oil, 1 tablespoon.

Black pepper, 1 teaspoon.

Salt as desired.

Garnishing with lemon peel (optional).

Preparation:

It is best to bring the olive oil to temperature in a frying pan set over medium-high heat.

Prepare the chicken breast strips in the oven until they are golden brown.

Salt, pepper, and chili sauce should be added. Stir thoroughly.

You should add the broccoli after it has been steaming for three to four minutes.

Put some basmati rice on each of the dishes so that it may be served.

Over the rice, pour the chicken and broccoli combination.

Lemon zest is a garnish (if desired).

Nutritional Plan (per serving):

Cal: about 460 Cal.

Fat: 11g (about 21% of total Cal.)

PROT: 30g (about 26% of total Cal.)

Carbs: 60g (about 53% of total Cal.)

Fiber: 5g (about 15% of total Cal.)

....

Barley Salad with Tomatoes and Cucumbers

Servings: 2
Ingredients

8 oz of cooked barley

4 oz cherry tomatoes, cut in half

4 oz cucumbers, diced

4 oz black olives, pitted

2 oz of crumbled feta cheese

Olive oil extra virgin, 2 tablespoons.

One lemon juice.

Oregano, dry, 1/2 teaspoon.

To taste, add salt and pepper.

Preparation:

Barley that has been cooked, cucumbers that have been chopped, black olives that have been pitted, and crumbled feta cheese should all be combined in a large bowl.

To prepare a vinaigrette, take a small bowl and mix together the extra virgin olive oil, lemon juice, dried oregano, and some salt and pepper.

After adding the vinaigrette, gently toss the salad.

Serve barley salad as a main meal or side dish.

Nutritional Plan (per serving):

Cal: about 380 Cal.

Fat: 14g (about 33% of total Cal.)

PROT: 9g (about 9% of total Cal.)

Carbs: 55g (about 58% of total Cal.)

Fiber: 8g (about 26% of total Cal.)

....

Smoked Salmon Bowl with Avocado and Brown Rice

Servings: 2
Ingredients

8 oz smoked salmon

4 oz cooked brown rice

1 avocado, sliced

4 oz cucumbers, diced

4 oz cherry tomatoes, cut in half

2 tbsp light mayonnaise

The juice of 1 lemon

Chopped chives for garnish (optional)

To taste, add salt and pepper.

Preparation:

Brown rice that has been cooked should be the foundation of a big bowl.

On top of the rice, arrange the smoked salmon, avocado slices, chopped cucumbers, and cherry tomatoes in half.

In order to make the sauce, mix the mayonnaise light, lemon juice, salt, and pepper together in a small bowl.

Pour the sauce over the contents of the bowl.

Garnish with chopped chives (if desired).

Nutritional Plan (per serving):

Cal: about 420 Cal.

Fat: 22g (about 47% of total Cal.)

PROT: 18g (about 17% of total Cal.)

Carbs: 41g (about 36% of total Cal.)

Fiber: 8g (about 28% of total Cal.)

....

Turkey Curry Meatballs with Couscous

Servings: 2
Ingredients

8 oz ground turkey meat

4 oz of cooked couscous

1 egg

2 tbsp wholemeal breadcrumbs

2 tbsp curry powder

Extra virgin olive oil, 1/2 tbsp.

To taste, add salt and pepper.

Serving of Greek yogurt (optional).

Preparation:

In a bowl, all of the following ingredients are mixed together: ground turkey meat, an egg, whole wheat bread crumbs, curry powder, salt, and pepper. Combine in great detail.

Make patties out of the mixture using your hands.

It is best to bring the olive oil to temperature in a frying pan set over medium-high heat.

The meatballs should be thoroughly cooked and evenly golden brown.

Meanwhile, prepare the cooked couscous as indicated in the instructions.

Serve the curried turkey meatballs over the couscous.

You can accompany the dish with Greek yogurt if you want a refreshing touch.

Nutritional Plan (per serving):

Cal: about 380 Cal.

Fat: 10g (about 24% of total Cal.)

PROT: 30g (about 31% of total Cal.)

Carbs: 44g (about 45% of total Cal.)

Fiber: 4g (about 13% of total Cal.)

....

Buckwheat Salad with Roasted Vegetables and Hummus

Servings: 2
Ingredients

8 oz of cooked buckwheat

4 oz of roasted, cut-into-strips red bell pepper

4 oz zucchini, diced and roasted

4 oz red onion, sliced and roasted

Cherry tomatoes, 4 ounces, split in half.

Hummus, 2 tablespoons.

Olive oil extra virgin, 2 tablespoons.

One lemon juice.

Chives, chopped, as a garnish (optional).

To taste, add salt and pepper.

Preparation:

A large bowl should be used to combine cooked buckwheat, roasted red peppers, roasted zucchini, roasted red onion, and cherry tomatoes that have been cut in half.

Vinaigrette can be made by combining extra virgin olive oil, lemon juice, salt, and pepper in a small bowl. This will create the dressing.

After adding the vinaigrette, gently toss the salad.

Serve buckwheat salad with hummus as a meal.

Nutritional Plan (per serving):

Cal: about 430 Cal.

Fat: 16g (about 33% of total Cal.)

PROT: 10g (about 9% of total Cal.)

Carbs: 63g (about 58% of total Cal.)

Fiber: 10g (about 33% of total Cal.)

....

CHAPTER 6:

Healthy Snacks

....

Guacamole with Whole Grain Corn Chips

Servings: 4
Ingredients

8 oz of mashed, peeled, and ripe avocado.

2 oz. of diced tomato.

2 oz. of finely sliced red onion.

1 ounce of chopped fresh cilantro.

One lime juice.

To taste, add salt and pepper.

4 oz whole grain corn chips to serve

Preparation:

The mashed avocado, tomato, red onion, and fresh cilantro should all be combined in a bowl.

When you have a guacamole that is smooth and creamy, add the lime juice, salt, and pepper and mix everything together thoroughly.

Serve the guacamole with whole-grain corn chips.

Nutritional Plan (per serving):

Cal: about 180 Cal.

Fat: 13g (about 65% of total Cal.)

PROT: 2g (about 4% of total Cal.)

Carbs: 16g (about 31% of total Cal.)

Fiber: 5g (about 20% of total Cal.)

....

Quinoa Bowl with Curried Tofu and Roasted Vegetables

Ingredients: (for Servings: 2)

4 oz extra-strong tofu, cut into cubes

1 C of cooked quinoa

1 round of zucchini, sliced.

Striped red bell pepper, one.

1 finely sliced carrot.

Curry powder, 1 teaspoon.

Extra virgin olive oil, 1 teaspoon.

One lemon juice.

To taste, add salt and pepper.

For garnish, use chopped walnuts and new parsley.

Preparation:

Put the oven temperature to 400 degrees Fahrenheit (200 degrees Celsius).

Mix the vegetables along with the olive oil, curry, salt, and pepper in a bowl before adding the peppers, zucchini, and carrots.

It is recommended that the vegetables be roasted in the oven for around 20 to 25 minutes or until they become tender and have a light brown color.

In the meantime, the tofu cubes should be cooked in a skillet that does not have a nonstick coating over medium-high heat until they are golden brown on all sides.

The quinoa that has been cooked, the roasted vegetables, and the tofu that has been curried should all be combined in a large bowl.

Squeeze the juice of half a lemon over the top and combine everything thoroughly.

Garnish your bowl with chopped walnuts and fresh parsley.

Serve hot as a main meal or side dish.

Nutritional Plan (per serving):

Cal: about 400 Cal.

Fat: 12g (around 27% of the total Cal.)

PROT: 18g (around 18% of the total Cal.)

Carbs: 56g (around 55% of the total Cal.)

Fiber: 10g (about 28% of total Cal.)

Tomato and Basil Crostini

Servings: 4
Ingredients

4 oz fresh tomatoes, diced

2 oz fresh basil, chopped

Olive oil extra virgin, 2 ounces.

1 minced garlic clove.

To taste, add salt and pepper.

8 slices of toasted whole wheat bread

Preparation:

In a bowl, all of the following ingredients should be mixed together: diced fresh tomatoes, chopped fresh basil, extra virgin olive oil, minced garlic, salt, and pepper. Combine in great detail.

Spread the tomato and basil mixture over the toasted bread slices.

Serve the croutons as appetizers.

Nutritional Plan (per serving):

Cal: about 120 Cal.

Fat: 7g (about 52% of total Cal.)

PROT: 2g (about 7% of total Cal.)

Carbs: 13g (about 41% of total Cal.)

Fiber: 2g (about 14% of total Cal.)

....

Soda Eggs with Hummus and Cherry Tomatoes

Servings: 4
Ingredients

8 oz hard-boiled eggs (2 eggs per serving)

4 oz of hummus

4 oz cherry tomatoes, cut in half

2 oz cucumbers, cut into rounds

Smoked paprika and chopped parsley for garnish (optional)

Preparation:

Cut the hard-boiled eggs in half after peeling.

Each egg half should have a spoonful of hummus on it.

Arrange the cherry tomatoes and cucumber slices next to the eggs.

Garnish with smoked paprika and chopped parsley (if desired).

Serve as appetizers.

Nutritional Plan (per serving):

Cal: about 140 Cal.

Fat: 9g (about 58% of total Cal.)

PROT: 6g (about 17% of total Cal.)

Carbs: 8g (about 24% of total Cal.)

Fiber: 2g (about 7% of total Cal.)

....

Bruschetta with Tomato and Mozzarella Cheese

Servings: 4
Ingredients

4 slices of toasted whole wheat bread

4 oz ripe, diced tomatoes

4 oz fresh mozzarella cheese, cut into cubes

2 oz fresh basil, chopped

Olive oil extra virgin, 2 ounces.

Peeled garlic clove number one.

To taste, add salt and pepper.

Preparation:

Lightly rub peeled garlic on toasted bread slices.

Mix tomatoes, fresh mozzarella, and chopped basil together in a bowl. Add the mixture to the bowl.

To season the mixture, salt, pepper, and extra virgin olive oil are utilized as seasonings.

Spread the tomato and mozzarella mix on the toasted bread slices.

Serve the bruschetta as an appetizer.

Nutritional Plan (per serving):

Cal: about 210 Cal.

Fat: 15g (around 64% of the total Cal.)

PROT: 7g (about 13% of total Cal.)

Carbs: 13g (about 24% of total Cal.)

Fiber: 2g (about 9% of total Cal.)

....

Roll of Smoked Salmon and Spreadable Cheese

Servings: 4
Ingredients

8 oz smoked salmon

4 oz of reduced-fat spreadable cheese

2 oz of cucumber, thinly sliced.

2 oz. of thinly sliced red bell pepper.

Chopped chives for garnish (optional)

Preparation:

A cutting board should have a slice of smoked salmon on it.

On top of each piece of salmon, apply one tablespoon of spreadable cheese.

Put a couple of strips of red bell pepper and cucumber in the middle of each slice.

Gently wrap the filling with the smoked salmon.

Cut each roll into small sections.

Garnish with chopped chives (if desired).

Serve the salmon rolls as appetizers.

Nutritional Plan (per serving):

Cal: about 120 Cal.

Fat: 6g (around 45% of the total Cal.)

PROT: 9g (around 30% of the total Cal.)

Carbs: 6g (around 25% of the total Cal.)

Fiber: 1g (about 4% of total Cal.)

....

Quinoa Meatballs with Yogurt Sauce

Servings: 4
Ingredients

8 oz of cooked quinoa

4 oz of crumbled feta cheese

2 oz. of finely sliced red onion.

2 oz of chopped fresh parsley.

1 egg.

Oatmeal, two tbsp worth.

To taste, add salt and pepper.

Natural Greek yogurt, 4 ounces, for the sauce.

Preparation:

In a bowl, we mix together oatmeal that has been cooked, crumbled feta cheese, red onion, fresh parsley, and quinoa that has been cooked. Combine in great detail.

Make patties out of the mixture using your hands.

A nonstick skillet should be heated up over medium-high heat and given a drizzle of oil.

Cook the patties in the pan until they are golden brown on all sides and cooked through completely.

A sauce is made by combining Greek yogurt, salt, and pepper in a small bowl. The end result is a sauce.

To serve, drizzle the yogurt sauce over the quinoa balls.

Nutritional Plan (per serving):
Cal: about 210 Cal.

Fat: 8g (about 34% of total Cal.)

PROT: 10g (around 19% of the total Cal.)

Carbs: 24g (about 47% of total Cal.)

Fiber: 3g (about 12% of total Cal.)

Fruit Skewers with Yogurt and Honey

Servings: 4
Ingredients

8 oz of strawberries

8 oz fresh pineapple

8 oz of red or green grapes

8 oz of natural Greek yogurt

2 oz of honey

4 skewer sticks

Preparation:

Cut the strawberries in half or quarters according to size.

Cut the pineapple into cubes.

Prepare skewers by alternating strawberries, pineapple chunks, and grapes.

Honey and Greek yogurt should be mixed together in a separate bowl.

Fruit skewers should be served alongside the dipping sauce made of yogurt and honey.

Nutritional Plan (per serving):

Cal: about 180 Cal.

Fat: 0.5g (about 3% of total Cal.)

PROT: 5g (about 11% of total Cal.)

Carbs: 42g (about 86% of total Cal.)

Fiber: 3g (around 10% of the total Cal.)

Mini Herb Omelettes

Servings: 4
Ingredients

4 oz of eggs (about 2 large eggs)

2 oz of skim milk

2 oz fresh spinach, chopped

2 oz of reduced-fat grated cheese (your choice)

2 oz of halves of cherry tomatoes.

1 ounce of finely sliced red onion.

For flavor, use fresh herbs like basil, parsley, and thyme.

Salt and pepper should be added to taste.

Use olive oil that is unfiltered and extra-virgin to grease the pan.

Preparation:

In a bowl, thoroughly combine the milk and eggs by beating them.

Include fresh herbs, chopped spinach, grated cheese, split cherry tomatoes, and chopped red onion, and season with salt and pepper to suit. Combine thoroughly.

A nonstick skillet ought to be oiled with a little bit of olive oil before being heated on a stovetop set to medium.

Pouring the egg mixture onto the hot pan will result in the creation of individual omelets.

The omelets should be cooked for a few minutes until golden brown and cooked throughout.

Serve the mini herb omelets as appetizers.

Nutritional Plan (per serving):
Cal: about 80 Cal.

Fat: 4g (about 45% of total Cal.)

PROT: 6g (around 32% of the total Cal.)

Carbs: 4g (about 23% of total Cal.)

Fiber: 1g (about 4% of total Cal.)

....

Guacamole with Vegetable Sticks
Servings: 4
Ingredients

8 oz of mashed, peeled, and ripe avocado.

2 oz. of diced tomato.

2 oz. of finely sliced red onion.

1 ounce of chopped fresh cilantro.

One lime juice.

To taste, add salt and pepper.

For serving, a mixture of vegetable sticks (carrots, celery, and peppers).

Preparation:

The mashed avocado, tomato, red onion, and fresh cilantro should all be combined in a bowl.

When you have a guacamole that is smooth and creamy, add the lime juice, salt, and pepper and mix everything together thoroughly.

Serve the guacamole with the mixed vegetable sticks.

Nutritional Plan (per serving):

Cal: about 180 Cal.

Fat: 13g (about 65% of total Cal.)

PROT: 2g (about 4% of total Cal.)

Carbs: 16g (about 31% of total Cal.)

Fiber: 5g (about 20% of total Cal.)

....

Eggplant Crostini alla Parmigiana

Servings: 4
Ingredients

8 oz eggplant, thinly sliced

4 oz of low-sodium marinara sauce

4 oz reduced-fat mozzarella cheese, grated

2 oz of chopped fresh basil.

To taste, add salt and pepper.

Olive oil extra virgin is used to grease the pan.

Slices of toasted whole wheat bread for serving

Preparation:

A nonstick skillet with a little olive oil in it should be heated to medium-high heat.

Slices of eggplant should be cooked until both sides are browned. To taste, add salt and pepper.

Take a piece of toast and cover it with some marinara sauce.

Place an eggplant slice on top of the sauce, then top with mozzarella cheese.

Create eggplant croutons by repeating the procedure.

Bake the croutons in a dish at a temperature of 350 degrees Fahrenheit (180 degrees Celsius) for approximately ten minutes or until the cheese has melted and turned golden.

To serve as an appetizer, garnish with fresh basil that has been chopped.

Nutritional Plan (per serving):

Cal: about 180 Cal.

Fat: 7g (about 35% of total Cal.)

PROT: 9g (about 20% of total Cal.)

Carbs: 20g (about 45% of total Cal.)

Fiber: 5g (about 19% of total Cal.)

....

Pea Guacamole with Corn Chips

Servings: 4
Ingredients

8 oz cooked green peas

2 oz. of finely sliced red onion.

1 ounce of chopped fresh cilantro.

One lime juice.

To taste, add salt and pepper.

4 oz whole grain corn chips to serve

Preparation:

Blend or process together the cooked green peas, minced red onion, fresh cilantro, lime juice, salt, and pepper in a food processor or blender.

Blend to the point where it reaches a creamy consistency.

Corn chips made with nutritious grains

should be served alongside the pea guacamole.

Nutritional Plan (per serving):

Cal: about 150 Cal.

Fat: 3g (about 18% of total Cal.)

PROT: 5g (about 14% of total Cal.)

Carbs: 26g (about 68% of total Cal.)

Fiber: 6g (about 24% of total Cal.)

....

Grilled Chicken Roll with Sweet Chili Sauce

Servings: 4
Ingredients

8 oz. of thinly sliced, grilled chicken breast.

2 oz. of thinly sliced red bell pepper.

2 oz of cucumber, thinly sliced.

2 oz of thinly sliced carrots.

2 oz of lettuce leaves.

4 sheets of rice spring roll wrappers (available at Asian grocery stores)

2 oz of sweet chili sauce (available in Asian grocery stores)

Preparation:

Prepare the rice spring roll rolls by following the instructions on the package.

In each roll sheet, place a lettuce leaf and add grilled chicken, red bell bell pepper, cucumber, and carrots.

Gently roll up each roll.

Cut each roulade in half diagonally.

Serve the grilled chicken rolls with the sweet chili sauce.

Nutritional Plan (per serving):

Cal: about 180 Cal.

Fat: 2g (about 10% of total Cal.)

PROT: 15g (about 33% of total Cal.)

Carbs: 29g (about 57% of total Cal.)

Fiber: 2g (about 8% of total Cal.)

....

Fruit Skewers with Yogurt and Mint Sauce

Servings: 4
Ingredients

8 oz of strawberries

8 oz fresh pineapple

8 oz of red or green grapes

8 oz of natural Greek yogurt

2 oz of honey

Fresh mint leaves for garnish

Preparation:

Cut the strawberries in half or quarters according to size.

Cut the pineapple into cubes.

Prepare skewers by alternating strawberries, pineapple chunks, and grapes.

In a low-calorie bowl, whisk together the honey and Greek yogurt.

The fruit skewers should be served with the yogurt sauce, and fresh mint leaves should be used as a garnish.

Nutritional Plan (per serving):

Cal: about 150 Cal.

Fat: 0.5g (about 3% of total Cal.)

PROT: 5g (about 13% of total Cal.)

Carbs: 34g (about 84% of total Cal.)

Fiber: 4g (about 14% of total Cal.)

Smoked Salmon and Cucumber Wrap

Servings: 4
Ingredients

8 oz smoked salmon

2 oz of reduced-fat spreadable cheese

1 cucumber, cut into thin strips

4 6-inch whole wheat tortillas

Chopped chives for garnish (optional)

Preparation:

Roll out a whole-wheat tortilla on a work surface.

Spread half an ounce of spreadable cheese on it.

Place two oz of smoked salmon in the center of the tortilla.

Add the cucumber strips.

Roll up the tortilla, forming a wrap.

Repeat the process to create the other wraps.

Cut each wrap diagonally in half.

Chives chopped for garnish (if desired).

Serve the smoked salmon wraps as appetizers.

Nutritional Plan (per serving):

Cal: about 160 Cal.

Fat: 6g (about 34% of total Cal.)

PROT: 8g (about 20% of total Cal.)

Carbs: 20g (about 46% of total Cal.)

Fiber: 4g (about 14% of total Cal.)

Chickpea Hummus with Vegetable Sticks

Servings: 4
Ingredients

8 oz cooked, rinsed and drained chickpeas

2 oz of lemon juice

2 oz tahini

Peeled garlic clove number one.

Two teaspoons of unrefined extra virgin olive oil.

Salt and pepper should be added to taste.

Mixed vegetable sticks (carrots, celery, peppers) for serving

Preparation:

Blend or process the cooked chickpeas, lemon juice, tahini, garlic clove, olive oil, salt, and pepper together in a food processor or blender.

Blend until the hummus attains a silky and creamy consistency. If additional water is needed to obtain the correct consistency, add it in at this point.

Serve the mixed veggie sticks with the chickpea hummus.

Nutritional Plan (per serving):

Cal: about 160 Cal.

Fat: 10g (about 56% of total Cal.)

PROT: 5g (about 13% of total Cal.)

Carbs: 15g (about 31% of total Cal.)

Fiber: 4g (about 15% of total Cal.)

....

Soda, Egg, and Avocado Salad

Servings: 4
Ingredients

8 oz hard-boiled eggs, cut into wedges

4 oz avocado, diced

2 oz of finely chopped red onion

2 oz., divided cherry tomatoes

2 oz cucumber, diced

2 tbsp light mayonnaise

1 tsp of mustard

To taste, add salt and pepper.

Preparation:

Eggs that have been hard-boiled and sliced, avocados that have been diced, red onion that has been chopped, cherry tomatoes that have been diced, and cucumber that has been diced should all be put in a large bowl.

To make the sauce, combine the light mayonnaise, mustard, salt, and pepper in a separate bowl. Stir to combine.

After adding the dressing, carefully toss the egg and avocado salad.

Serve the boiled egg and avocado salad as an appetizer.

Nutritional Plan (per serving):

Cal: about 200 Cal.

Fat: 14g (about 63% of total Cal.)

PROT: 7g (about 14% of total Cal.)

Carbs: 12g (about 24% of total Cal.)

Fiber: 4g (about 16% of total Cal.)

....

Bruschetta with Tomatoes and Basil

Servings: 4
Ingredients

8 oz ripe, diced tomatoes

2 oz fresh basil, chopped

2 oz red onion, finely chopped

Olive oil extra virgin, 2 tablespoons.

Peeled garlic clove number one.

To taste, add salt and pepper.

Toasty whole wheat bread in four slices.

Preparation:

In a bowl, combine the diced tomatoes, the chopped fresh basil, the chopped red onion, the olive oil, and a full clove of garlic (which you may remove before serving). Season with salt and pepper.

Mix the ingredients well to season the tomatoes.

Toast slices of whole wheat bread.

When the bread is toasted, rub garlic on each slice to impart a subtle aroma.

Spread the tomato and basil dressing over the toasted bread slices.

Serve the bruschetta with tomatoes and basil as appetizers.

Nutritional Plan (per serving):

Cal: about 150 Cal.

Fat: 7g (about 42% of total Cal.)

PROT: 4g (about 10% of total Cal.)

Carbs: 20g (about 48% of total Cal.)

Fiber: 4g (about 16% of total Cal.)

....

Melon with Ham

Servings: 4
Ingredients

8 oz ripe melon, cut into cubes or balls

4 oz of prosciutto, cut into thin strips

Leaves of fresh mint used as a garnish (optional)

Preparation:

Prepare the melon by cutting it into cubes or using a digger to create spheres.

Wrap each piece of melon with a strip of prosciutto.

Garnish with fresh mint leaves (if desired).

Serve melon with prosciutto as an appetizer.

Nutritional Plan (per serving):
Cal: about 60 Cal.

Fat: 2g (about 30% of total Cal.)

PROT: 4g (about 27% of total Cal.)

Carbs: 7g (about 43% of total Cal.)

Fiber: 1g (about 10% of total Cal.)

Beet Hummus with Vegetable Sticks

Servings: 4
Ingredients

8 oz cooked and peeled beets

2 oz cooked, rinsed, and drained chickpeas

1 oz of lemon juice

Peeled garlic clove number one.

Two teaspoons of unrefined extra virgin olive oil.

Salt and pepper should be added to taste.

Mixed vegetable sticks (carrots, celery, peppers) for serving

Preparation:

In a blender or food processor, combine the cooked beets, cooked chickpeas, lemon juice, garlic clove, olive oil, salt, and pepper.

Blend until the hummus attains a silky and creamy consistency. If additional water is needed to obtain the correct consistency, add it in at this point.

Serve the beet hummus with the mixed vegetable sticks.

Nutritional Plan (per serving):

Cal: about 150 Cal.

Fat: 7g (about 42% of total Cal.)

PROT: 4g (about 10% of total Cal.)

Carbs: 18g (about 48% of total Cal.)

Fiber: 4g (about 16% of total Cal.)

Mini Frittatas with Tomato and Basil

Servings: 4
Ingredients

4 oz ripe, diced tomatoes

2 oz fresh basil, chopped

4 eggs

Milk, 2 tablespoons.

To taste, add salt and pepper.

Olive oil extra virgin, 2 tablespoons.

Preparation:

In a bowl, beat the eggs with the milk, then add the seasonings of your choice, finishing with the finely chopped fresh basil.

Olive oil should be heated over medium-high heat in a skillet that does not stick.

After the omelets have been prepared, fill them with the egg mixture and fry them for two to three minutes on one side.

Tomato cubes should be added to the small frittatas.

The small frittatas should be cooked for a further 2 to 3 minutes or until well cooked, using a lid or plate.

As an appetizer, provide the little tomato-basil frittatas.

Nutritional Plan (per serving):
Cal: about 120 Cal.

Fat: 8g (around 60% of total Cal.)

PROT: 6g (around 20% of the total Cal.)

Carbs: 4g (about 20% of total Cal.)

Fiber: 1g (about 5% of total Cal.)

Crostini with Goat's Cheese and Honey

Servings: 4
Ingredients

4 oz of goat cheese

2 oz of honey

8 slices of toasted whole wheat bread

Chopped walnuts for garnish (optional)

Preparation:

Spread a slice of toasted whole-wheat bread on a plate.

Spread an ounce of goat cheese on the slice of bread.

Pour a little honey over the cheese.

Garnish with chopped walnuts (if desired).

Repeat the process to create the other croutons.

Serve the croutons with goat cheese and honey as an appetizer.

Nutritional Plan (per serving):

Cal: about 200 Cal.

Fat: 7g (about 31% of total Cal.)

PROT: 6g (about 12% of total Cal.)

Carbs: 30g (about 57% of total Cal.)

Fiber: 3g (about 12% of total Cal.)

Grilled Chicken Skewers with Yogurt and Mint Sauce

Servings: 4
Ingredients

8 oz grilled chicken breast, diced

2 oz of natural Greek yogurt

2 oz fresh mint, chopped

1 garlic clove, minced finely.

To taste, add salt and pepper.

Skewer sticks.

Preparation:

In order to make the sauce, put some Greek yogurt in a bowl and add some fresh mint leaves, a clove of garlic, some salt, and some pepper.

Chicken cubes are threaded onto skewer rods.

Grill the chicken skewers until they are well cooked.

Serve the grilled chicken skewers with the yogurt and mint sauce as an appetizer.

Nutritional Plan (per serving):

Cal: about 180 Cal.

Fat: 5g (about 25% of total Cal.)

PROT: 26g (about 58% of total Cal.)

Carbs: 4g (about 9% of total Cal.)

Fiber: 1g (about 4% of total Cal.)

Mackerel with Orange and Ginger

Servings: 4
Ingredients

16 oz of mackerel fillets

2 oz of orange juice

1 tsp fresh grated ginger

1 garlic clove, minced finely.

To taste, add salt and pepper.

Preparation:

In a bowl, add orange juice, ginger that has been grated, garlic that has been minced, salt, and pepper to form the marinade.

After positioning the mackerel fillets in an oven tray, proceed to pour the marinade over top of them.

Cover the dish and place it in the refrigerator to marinate for at least thirty minutes.

The mackerel fillets should be grilled for three to four minutes on each side or until the fish reaches an internal temperature of 145 degrees Fahrenheit.

Serve orange and ginger mackerel as an appetizer.

Nutritional Plan (per serving):

Cal: about 200 Cal.

Fat: 12g (about 54% of total Cal.)

PROT: 22g (about 44% of total Cal.)

Carbs: 4g (about 8% of total Cal.)

Fiber: 0g

....

Seaweed and Cucumber Salad

Servings: 4
Ingredients

4 oz of dried wakame seaweed

2 oz cucumber, cut into thin strips

2 oz. of finely sliced red onion.

Rice vinegar, 2 oz.

1 sugar teaspoon.

One tbsp of toasted sesame oil.

Garnish: toasted sesame seeds (optional).

Preparation:

The dried wakame seaweed should be submerged in a big basin of cold water. Soak them for about five minutes or until they are soft. Well-drain and squeeze them.

Combine red onion, cucumber strips, and wakame seaweed that has been rehydrated in a bowl.

In a smaller bowl, add the rice vinegar, sugar, and sesame oil. Stir the mixture occasionally until the sugar is completely dissolved.

Mix thoroughly after adding the dressing to the seaweed salad.

Add toasted sesame seeds as a garnish (if desired).

Serve the seaweed and cucumber salad as an appetizer.

Nutritional Plan (per serving):

Cal: about 60 Cal.

Fat: 1g (about 15% of total Cal.)

PROT: 2g (about 13% of total Cal.)

Carbs: 12g (about 72% of total Cal.)

Fiber: 2g (about 8% of total Cal.)

....

Baked Zucchini Fries

Servings: 4

Ingredients

16 oz of thinly sliced zucchini.

Extra virgin olive oil, 1 ounce.

Smoked paprika, 1 teaspoon.

To taste, add salt and pepper.

Preparation:

Turn the oven up to 425 degrees Fahrenheit (220 degrees Celsius).

In a bowl, zucchini slices should be tossed with olive oil, smoked paprika, salt, and pepper before being served.

Arrange the sliced zucchini in a single layer on a baking sheet that has been covered with parchment paper.

Bake the zucchini chips for 15 to 20 minutes or until they have achieved the desired crispiness and light browning.

Serve baked zucchini fries as an appetizer.

Nutritional Plan (per serving):

Cal: about 50 Cal.

Fat: 4g (about 72% of total Cal.)

PROT: 1g (about 8% of total Cal.)

Carbs: 4g (about 20% of total Cal.)

Fiber: 1g (about 4% of total Cal.)

Beet Carpaccio with Walnuts and Goat's Cheese

Servings: 4
Ingredients

12 oz thinly sliced red beets

2 oz roasted walnuts, chopped

2 oz goat cheese, crumbled

Extra virgin olive oil, 1 tablespoon.

One lemon juice.

To taste, add salt and pepper.

For garnish, use arugula.

Preparation:

Arrange the thin slices of beets on a serving platter.

Be sure to use olive oil and lemon juice when preparing the beets.

Scatter chopped walnuts and crumbled goat cheese over the beets.

To taste, add salt and pepper.

Arugula leaves are a good garnish.

Serve the beet carpaccio as an appetizer.

Nutritional Plan (per serving):

Cal: about 180 Cal.

Fat: 12g (about 60% of total Cal.)

PROT: 6g (about 13% of total Cal.)

Carbs: 14g (about 27% of total Cal.)

Fiber: 4g (about 16% of total Cal.)

Quinoa with Turmeric Chicken and Roasted Vegetables

Ingredients: Servings: 4

8 oz (about 1 cup) of skinless, diced chicken breasts

1 C of quinoa

2 C of vegetable broth

1 tbsp olive oil (about 0.5 oz)

1 tsp turmeric powder

1 tsp sweet paprika

2 medium carrots, cut very thin (about 8 oz).

Thinly sliced 1 medium zucchini (about 6 oz).

A single red bell pepper, thinly sliced (about 6 oz).

To taste, add salt and black pepper.

Fresh parsley, chopped, as a garnish (optional).

Preparation:

Set the oven to 200 °C or 400 °F.

In a bowl, give the quinoa a quick rinsing with some lukewarm water. Then, bring the vegetable broth to a boil in a saucepan before adding the quinoa. After the quinoa has soaked up the liquid and become pliable, cover the pan, turn the heat down to low, and allow the mixture to simmer for about 15 minutes.

During the time that the quinoa is being cooked, the chicken is diced and mixed in a bowl with turmeric, sweet paprika, salt, and black pepper.

On a baking sheet lined with parchment paper, give the chicken that has been marinated 15 to 20 minutes in the oven or until it is cooked all the way through and has a golden brown color.

While the chicken is cooking, prepare the carrot, zucchini, and red bell pepper slices and spread them out in a separate baking dish. To taste, add a pinch each of salt and black pepper, as well as a few drops of olive oil. It is recommended that the veggies be roasted for fifteen to twenty minutes or until they have become soft and have a light caramelization.

When ready, combine the cooked quinoa with the roasted vegetables.

Serve the quinoa and vegetable mix on four plates and garnish with the turmeric chicken. If desired, add some chopped fresh parsley on top.

Nutritional Plan (per serving):

Cal: about 350 Cal.

Fat: 7g (about 18% of total Cal.)

PROT: 25g (about 29% of total Cal.)

Carbs: 47g (about 53% of total Cal.)

Fiber: 6g

....

Eggs Stuffed with Smoked Salmon and Dill

Servings: 4
Ingredients

4 halves of hard-boiled eggs and

2 thin pieces of cured salmon

2 oz of light spreadable cheese

Fresh dill for garnish (optional)

To taste, add salt and pepper.

Preparation:

Hard-boiled egg yolks should be removed and put in a bowl.

The egg yolks and light spreadable cheese should be combined thoroughly until the mixture has a creamy texture.

Fill the hard-boiled egg halves with the cheese and yolk mixture.

Add strips of smoked salmon on top of each stuffed egg.

Salt and pepper should be added to taste.

Fresh dill can be used as a garnish if desired.

Serve the eggs stuffed with smoked salmon as an appetizer.

Nutritional Plan (per serving):

Cal: about 90 Cal.

Fat: 6g (about 60% of total Cal.)

PROT: 8g (about 36% of total Cal.)

Carbs: 1g (about 4% of total Cal.)

Fiber: 0g

....

CHAPTER 7:

Light and Tasty Dinners

....

Steamed Salmon with Broccoli and Dill Sauce

Servings: 2
Ingredients

2 fillets of salmon (about 6 oz each).

8 oz of chopped-up broccoli.

Lemon juice and 2 tsp of chopped fresh dill.

To taste, add salt and pepper.

Preparation:

Prepare a steam pot.

The salmon fillets are seasoned with lemon juice, salt, and pepper before being baked.

The salmon should be done after 10 to 12 minutes of steaming.

Meanwhile, steam broccoli until tender.

Serve the salmon with the broccoli and sprinkle with fresh dill.

Nutritional Plan (per serving):

Cal: about 250 Cal.

Fat: 14g (about 50% of total Cal.)

PROT: 28g (about 45% of total Cal.)

Carbs: 10g (about 15% of total Cal.)

Fiber: 4g (about 16% of total Cal.)

....

Grilled Chicken Breast with Lemon and Capers Sauce

Servings: 2
Ingredients

2 chicken breasts (about 6 oz each)

2 oz of lemon juice

1 oz capers, rinsed

Extra virgin olive oil, 1 tablespoon

To taste, add salt and pepper.

Preparation:

Grill the chicken breasts over high heat until thoroughly cooked.

To prepare the sauce, take a small bowl and mix together the lemon juice, capers, olive oil, and seasonings (salt and pepper).

The lemon caper sauce should be served alongside the grilled chicken breasts.

Nutritional Plan (per serving):

Cal: about 250 Cal.

Fat: 9g (about 32% of total Cal.)

PROT: 36g (about 58% of total Cal.)

Carbs: 4g (about 6% of total Cal.)

Fiber: 1g (about 4% of total Cal.)

....

Curried Tofu with Vegetables

Servings: 2
Ingredients

8 oz tofu, cut into cubes

4 oz broccoli, divided into florets

4 oz of red bell pepper, thinly sliced

2 oz of coconut milk

1 tbsp of curry paste

1 tbsp extra virgin olive oil

To taste, add salt and pepper.

Preparation:

Olive oil is heated in a nonstick skillet before the tofu cubes are added. Cook until they are evenly golden brown.

Cook the broccoli and red peppers after adding them.

Curry paste and coconut milk should be combined in a bowl. Put the tofu and vegetables in the pan and carefully pour this mixture in.

Cook for a few minutes until the sauce thickens.

Serve curried tofu with vegetables as a light dinner.

Nutritional Plan (per serving):

Cal: about 350 Cal.

Fat: 22g (about 56% of total Cal.)

PROT: 16g (about 18% of total Cal.)

Carbs: 22g (about 26% of total Cal.)

Fiber: 7g (about 25% of total Cal.)

....

Chickpea and Tomato Salad with Tuna

Servings: 2
Ingredients

8 oz cooked chickpeas (rinsed and drained)

4 oz cherry tomatoes, cut in half

4 oz canned tuna, drained

Lemon juice and

two tsp of extra virgin olive oil

Chopped fresh parsley for garnish (optional)

Salt and pepper to taste.

Preparation:

It is recommended that the chickpeas, cherry tomatoes, and tuna all be mixed together in a dish.

Season the dish with salt, pepper, lemon juice, and olive oil, and then add these ingredients.

Garnish with fresh chopped parsley (if desired).

Serve chickpea and tomato salad with tuna as a light dinner.

Nutritional Plan (per serving):

Cal: about 350 Cal.

Fat: 14g (about 36% of total Cal.)

PROT: 22g (about 25% of total Cal.)

Carbs: 37g (about 39% of total Cal.)

Fiber: 10g (about 35% of total Cal.)

....

Salmon Salad with Avocado and Asparagus

Ingredients: Servings: 4

16 oz (about 4 fillets) of fresh salmon

2 ripe avocados, cut into cubes

2-inch chunks of one bunch of asparagus

4 C fresh spinach (about 4 oz)

1/4 C toasted pecans, chopped (about 1 oz)

Two tablespoons of extra-virgin olive oil (about 1 oz).

The lemon juice is extracted from one (about 2 oz).

Salt and black pepper should be added to taste.

Preparation:

Put the oven temperature to about 392 degrees Fahrenheit (200 degrees Celsius).

Arrange the salmon fillets in a single layer on a baking sheet that has been covered with baking paper. To season them, add some salt, pepper, and a very small amount of olive oil. Bake the salmon in the oven that has been preheated for 12 to 15 minutes or until the flesh of the fish can be easily flaked apart with a fork.

While the salmon is cooking, bring some water to a boil in a separate saucepan. Cook the asparagus in water that is boiling for three to four minutes or until it reaches the desired tenderness. After they have been drained, place them straight away in ice water to stop the cooking process. Because of this, they will maintain their transparency and brilliance.

In a large bowl, combine the fresh spinach, the juice of half a lemon, and one tablespoon of olive oil. Salt and pepper should be added to taste.

After placing the salad on each tray, it can then be served.

Salmon that has been cooked should be placed on top of the spinach salad.

Arrange the cooked asparagus and avocado cubes on top of the salmon to create a beautiful presentation.

To finish, sprinkle the top with toasted pecans.

Add a finishing touch to the dish by drizzling it with extra virgin olive oil.

Nutritional Plan (per serving):

Cal: about 400 Cal.

Fat: 30g (around 66% of total Cal.)

PROT: 30g (around 30% of the total Cal.)

Carbs: 14g (around 14% of the total Cal.)

Fiber: 9g

Tofu Tacos with Avocado Sauce

Servings: 2
Ingredients

6 oz tofu, cut into thin strips

4 oz ripe avocado, mashed

2 oz tomato, diced

2 oz. of finely sliced red onion.

Lime juice, 1 ounce.

1 ounce of chopped fresh cilantro.

Extra virgin olive oil, 1 teaspoon.

Smoked paprika, 1 teaspoon.

To taste, add salt and pepper.

Taco shells made of whole grain for serving.

Preparation:

Cook the tofu strips in the heated olive oil until they turn a golden brown color.

To prepare the sauce, take a bowl and mix together the following ingredients: crushed avocado, chopped tomato, diced red onion, fresh cilantro, lime juice, smoked paprika, salt, and pepper.

Fill the whole-wheat taco shells with the grilled tofu strips and avocado salsa.

Serve tofu tacos with avocado salsa as a light dinner.

Nutritional Plan (per serving):

Cal: about 300 Cal.

Fat: 16g (about 48% of total Cal.)

PROT: 14g (about 19% of total Cal.)

Carbs: 28g (about 33% of total Cal.)

Fiber: 8g (about 32% of total Cal.)

Roast Chicken with Sweet Potatoes and Vegetables

Servings: 2
Ingredients

12 oz of chicken breast

8 oz sweet potatoes, diced

4 oz zucchini, cut into rounds

2 oz. of thinly sliced red bell pepper.

Extra virgin olive oil, 1 tablespoon.

One tbsp of dried oregano.

To taste, add salt and pepper.

Preparation:

Put the oven temperature to 400 degrees Fahrenheit (200 degrees Celsius).

In a bowl, combine the zucchini, peppers, and sweet potatoes with the oregano, olive oil, and salt.

Arrange the vegetables in a single layer on a baking sheet that has been covered with parchment paper.

It is recommended that the chicken breast be seasoned with salt, pepper, and olive oil before cooking.

Place the chicken breasts on the baking sheet that was also used for the vegetables.

Bake for approximately 20 to 25 minutes, or until the vegetables have reached the desired consistency and the chicken is cooked through.

As a light dinner, serve roast chicken with sweet potatoes and vegetables.

Nutritional Plan (per serving):

Cal: about 350 Cal.

Fat: 9g (about 23% of total Cal.)

PROT: 30g (about 35% of total Cal.)

Carbs: 40g (about 42% of total Cal.)

Fiber: 8g (about 32% of total Cal.)

Spinach Salad with Grilled Salmon and Almonds

Servings: 2
Ingredients

8 oz grilled salmon (2 fillets, 4 oz each)

4 oz of fresh spinach

1 oz toasted almonds, chopped

Olive oil extra virgin, 2 tablespoons.

One lemon juice.

To taste, add salt and pepper.

Preparation:

Heat a grill and cook the salmon until well done.

Fresh spinach, sliced almonds, olive oil, and lemon juice are all put in a bowl.

After seasoning with salt and pepper to taste, thoroughly combine the ingredients.

On top of the salad, scatter the chunks of cooked salmon that have been cut into pieces.

Serve spinach salad with grilled salmon as a light dinner.

Nutritional Plan (per serving):

Cal: about 320 Cal.

Fat: 23g (about 64% of total Cal.)

PROT: 23g (about 29% of total Cal.)

Carbs: 10g (about 12% of total Cal.)

Fiber: 4g (about 15% of total Cal.)

....

Curried Tofu Bowl with Quinoa and Roasted Vegetables

Ingredients: Servings: 4

12 oz (about 340g) of extra-strong tofu, cut into cubes

1 C of quinoa (about 6 oz), rinsed and drained

2 C of broccoli (about 8 oz), divided into small florets

2 medium carrots, thinly sliced (approximately 6 oz).

Extra virgin olive oil, 1 tbsp (about 0.5 oz).

One tsp of curry powder.

A half-teaspoon of paprika.

To taste, add salt and black pepper.

For garnish, add 1/4 C finely chopped fresh cilantro (approximately 0.5 ounce).

For the Curry Sauce:

1/2 C Greek yogurt (about 4 oz)

1 tbsp of honey (about 0.5 oz)

1 tsp curry powder

1 lime's juice (about 2 oz)

To taste, add salt and black pepper.

Preparation:

Preheat the oven to 200 degrees Celsius, which is roughly 392 degrees Fahrenheit.

Tofu that has been diced and mixed in a bowl with olive oil, curry powder, paprika, salt, and pepper.

Place the tofu that has been marinated on a baking sheet that has been covered with parchment paper. Bake the tofu in an oven that has been warmed for 25 to 30 minutes, turning them over once in the middle of the cooking process or until they are golden brown.

In the meantime, prepare the quinoa by cooking it according to the directions on the package.

Place the broccoli and carrots in a separate baking dish, and then season them with salt, pepper, and a dash of olive oil. Bake until the vegetables are tender. If you want crisp vegetables that are still tender inside, cook the vegetables in the oven for 20 to 25 minutes.

The curry sauce is made by mixing together in a bowl Greek yogurt, honey, curry powder, lime juice, salt, and black pepper.

Spread the quinoa out on plates before serving. Place the roasted veggies in a serving dish, then cover with the curry sauce.

Complete the dish with chopped fresh cilantro.

Nutritional Plan (per serving):

Cal: about 420 Cal.

Fat: 14g (about 30% of total Cal.)

PROT: 19g (about 18% of total Cal.)

Carbs: 58g (about 52% of total Cal.)

Fiber: 9g

....

Steamed Salmon with Lemon Dill Sauce

Ingredients: Servings: 2

2 salmon fillets (about 6 oz each)

2 tbsp of lemon juice that is fresh.

1 tsp of lemon peel, shredded.

2 tbsp chopped fresh dill.

Quarter C fish stock (without salt).

To taste, add salt and black pepper.

Preparation:

Prepare the lemon-dill sauce first. Combine fresh lemon juice, grated lemon peel, and chopped dill in a small bowl. Place aside.

A tiny amount of water in a saucepan should be heated until it just begins to boil, then the heat should be lowered to medium-low.

Put the salmon fillets in a steamer basket, then set the basket on top of the pot. The salmon should not come into contact with the water at any point during the cooking process. Place the lid on top of the pot.

Steam the salmon for eight to ten minutes or until it easily flakes apart when examined with a fork, whichever comes first.

While the salmon is cooking, bring the fish stock to a simmer in a small skillet over medium-low heat. Before adding the lemon-dill sauce that had been created earlier, give it a good stir. Prepare the sauce by bringing it to a simmer for a few minutes.

Transfer the cooked salmon to the serving dishes in a gentle manner. Pour the lemon-dill sauce over the fish before serving. Salt and pepper should be added to taste.

Serve steamed salmon with vegetable sides or salad for a light, anti-inflammatory dinner.

Nutritional Plan (per serving):

Cal: about 220 Cal.

Fat: 10g (about 41% of total Cal.)

PROT: 29g (about 53% of total Cal.)

Carbs: 3g (about 6% of total Cal.)

Fiber: 0g

....

Grilled Chicken with Lemon and caper sauce

Servings: 2
Ingredients

2 chicken breasts (about 6 oz each)

1 oz of lemon juice

1 oz capers, rinsed

Extra virgin olive oil, 1 tablespoon.

To taste, add salt and pepper.

Fresh parsley, chopped, as a garnish (optional).

Preparation:

Heat a grill and cook the chicken breasts until well done.

To prepare the sauce, take a small bowl and mix together the lemon juice, capers, olive oil, and seasonings (salt and pepper).

Serve the lemon caper sauce beside the cooked chicken breast.

Add freshly cut parsley as a garnish (if desired).

Nutritional Plan (per serving):

Cal: about 250 Cal.

Fat: 9g (about 32% of total Cal.)

PROT: 36g (about 58% of total Cal.)

Carbs: 4g (about 6% of total Cal.)

Fiber: 1g (about 4% of total Cal.)

....

Grilled Salmon with Turmeric Sauce

Ingredients (for 2 servings):

2 salmon fillets (4-6 oz each)

1 tbsp extra virgin olive oil

1 tsp of powdered turmeric.

1/2 of a tsp of sweet paprika.

One-half tsp of garlic powder.

To taste, add salt and black pepper.

One lemon juice.

Lemon zest was grated.

Fresh parsley for garnish

For the Sauce:

1/4 C of natural Greek yogurt

1 tsp turmeric powder

Juice of 1/2 lemon

To taste, add salt and pepper.

Preparation:

Set the grill's temperature to medium-high.

Olive oil, turmeric, sweet paprika, garlic powder, grated lemon zest, lemon juice, and salt and pepper should all be mixed together in a bowl before proceeding.

Apply this marinade to the salmon fillets, and then set them aside to rest for approximately ten minutes.

While the salmon is resting, you may prepare the sauce. In a bowl, mix together the turmeric, salt, and pepper, along with the Greek yogurt, lemon juice, and salt.

It is recommended that you grill the salmon for three to four minutes on each side or until it can be easily flaked with a fork.

The grilled salmon should be topped with fresh parsley and the turmeric sauce before serving.

Nutritional Plan (per serving):

Cal: about 350 Cal.

Fat: 18g (about 49% of total Cal.)

PROT: 36g (about 41% of total Cal.)

Carbs: 10g (about 10% of total Cal.)

Fiber: 2g (about 7% of total Cal.)

Salmon Salad with Cucumbers and Lemon Yogurt Dressing

Ingredients: Servings: 4

16 oz (4 fillets) of fresh, cooked and shelled salmon

2 cucumbers, thinly sliced (about 8 oz)

1 C of Greek yogurt (about 8 oz)

Juice of 1 lemon (about 2 oz)

Grated zest of 1 lemon

2 tbsp chopped fresh chives (about 0.5 oz)

To taste, add salt and black pepper.

Green salad to taste to accompany (about 4 cups)

1 tbsp olive oil (about 0.5 oz)

Preparation:

Greek yoghurt, lemon juice, grated lemon zest, and chopped chives should be combined in a bowl. Salt and black pepper should be added to taste. This will be the sauce made with lemon yogurt.

Slices of cucumber and olive oil should be combined in another bowl. To season the cucumbers, sprinkle on some black pepper and a dash of salt.

Distribute the green salad among four plates.

One salmon fillet should be placed above the salad on each individual plate.

Over the salmon fillets, evenly distribute the lemon yogurt sauce.

Garnish each plate with the marinated cucumber slices.

Serve immediately and enjoy this fresh and tasty salmon salad.

Nutritional Plan (per serving):

Cal: about 300 Cal.

Fat: 13g (about 39% of total Cal.)

PROT: 32g (about 43% of total Cal.)

Carbs: 14g (about 18% of total Cal.)

Fiber: 2g

Tomato and Cucumber Quinoa Salad with Lemon Yogurt Dressing

Ingredients: Servings: 4

1 C of quinoa (about 6 oz), rinsed and drained

2 C cherry tomatoes, cut in half (about 10 oz)

2 cucumbers, diced (about 12 oz)

1/2 C coarsely chopped red onion (about 3 oz)

1/4 C fresh basil, chopped (about 0.5 oz)

1/4 C fresh parsley, chopped (about 0.5 oz)

1/4 C fresh mint, chopped (about 0.5 oz)

Greek yogurt, half a C (about 4 oz).

Lemon juice from one (about 2 oz).

Olive oil extra virgin, 2 tbsp(about 1 oz).

To taste, add salt and black pepper.

Preparation:

Cook the quinoa in a pot according to the directions on the package. After cooking, place it in a sizable bowl and allow it to cool.

Add the halved cherry tomatoes, diced cucumbers, chopped red onion, basil, parsley, and mint to the cooled quinoa. Mix all ingredients well.

In a separate bowl, mix together Greek yogurt, lemon juice, olive oil, salt, and black pepper to make the lemon yogurt sauce. Make sure the sauce is completely smooth by stirring it.

To uniformly distribute the yogurt sauce, pour it over the quinoa and vegetables and gently mix.

Serve tomato and cucumber quinoa salad as a light and refreshing meal.

Nutritional Plan (per serving):

Cal: about 280 Cal.

Fat: 9g (about 29% of total Cal.)

PROT: 9g (about 13% of total Cal.)

Carbs: 44g (about 58% of total Cal.)

Fiber: 7g

Baked Salmon with Lemon Quinoa and Spinach

Servings: 2
Ingredients

2 fillets of salmon (about 6 oz each)

4 oz of cooked quinoa

4 oz of fresh spinach

one lemon juice.

Extra virgin olive oil, 1 tablespoon.

To taste, add salt and pepper.

Preparation:

Turn the temperature dial on the oven to 400 degrees Fahrenheit (200 degrees Celsius).

The salmon fillets need to be placed on a baking tray that has been covered with parchment paper.

In order to season the fish, lemon juice, olive oil, salt, and pepper are utilized.

Cooking time for the salmon should be approximately 15 to 20 minutes in the oven.

Meanwhile, in a bowl, mix the cooked quinoa and fresh spinach.

When the salmon is ready, serve over the quinoa and spinach mixture.

Nutritional Plan (per serving):

Cal: about 350 Cal.

Fat: 13g (around 33% of the total Cal.)

PROT: 32g (around 37% of the total Cal.)

Carbs: 25g (around 30% of the total Cal.)

Fiber: 4g (about 16% of total Cal.)

....

Grilled Quinoa and Zucchini Salad with Lemon Mint Dressing

Ingredients: Servings: 4

Quinoa, 1 cup.

Water, 2 cups.

2 medium zucchini, each weighing around 7 oz, finely cut.

Olive oil, 1/4 cup.

2 tbsp of lemon juice that is fresh.

1 tsp of lemon peel, shredded.

2 tsp of finely chopped fresh mint leaves.

To taste, add salt and black pepper.

Preparation:

First, get the quinoa ready to eat. Rinse the quinoa very well in water that is both chilly and flowing. It needs to be cooked in a pot that has some salt and two cups of water added to it. After the quinoa has been cooked and the water has been absorbed, bring the mixture to a boil, after which you should cover the pot, reduce the heat to a low setting, and allow it to simmer for 15 to 20 minutes.

When it is ready, remove the food from the heat and allow it to cool.

While the quinoa is cooling, preheat a grill or skillet that does not require oil over medium-high heat. Before placing zucchini slices on the grill, a light coating of olive oil should be applied to each side of the slices. The zucchini should be grilled for two to three minutes per side or until it is tender and has scored throughout. They have reached the end of their cooking time and should be removed from the grill.

In a low-sided bowl or saucepan, make the lemon-mint sauce. To taste, incorporate some olive oil, fresh lemon juice, grated lemon peel, finely chopped mint, and a pinch each of salt and black pepper.

In a large bowl, combine the quinoa that has been cooked and allow it to cool with the grilled zucchini slices.

Mix the quinoa and zucchini thoroughly before adding the lemon-mint dressing on top.

As a side dish or main meal, serve the salad. It can be kept in the fridge for a quick lunch the following day.

Nutritional Plan (per serving):

Cal: about 270 Cal.

Fat: 12g (about 40% of total Cal.)

PROT: 7g (about 10% of total Cal.)

Carbs: 35g (about 50% of total Cal.)

Fiber: 5g

....

Quinoa and Beet Salad with Cumin Hummus

Ingredients: Servings: 4

1 C cooked and cooled quinoa (6 oz)

2 medium beets, cooked and diced (8 oz)

1 cucumber, diced (4 oz)

1/4 C cumin hummus (2 oz)

One lemon juice.

Olive oil, two tbsp(1 oz).

2 tsp chopped fresh parsley (0.5 oz).

To taste, add salt and black pepper.

Garnish: toasted sesame seeds (optional).

Preparation:

In a sizable bowl, mix together diced beets, cucumber, and quinoa that have been previously cooked.

Vinaigrette can be made by combining cumin hummus, lemon juice, olive oil, finely chopped fresh parsley, freshly ground black pepper, and salt in a small bowl. This will generate the vinaigrette. Mix all of the ingredients thoroughly until they are smooth.

After that, give the contents of the large dish with the vinaigrette a little toss until all of the components have an equivalent amount of seasoning.

To further improve the flavor, season to taste with salt and black pepper.

If desired, garnish with toasted sesame seeds for a crunchy touch.

Serve quinoa and beet salad as a light and tasty meal.

Nutritional Plan (per serving):

Cal: about 260 Cal.

Fat: 10g (about 34% of total Cal.)

PROT: 8g (about 12% of total Cal.)

Carbs: 36g (about 54% of total Cal.)

Fiber: 6g

....

Salmon Curry with Quinoa and Broccoli

Ingredients: Servings: 4

4 salmon fillets (about 16 oz)

1 C of quinoa (about 4 oz)

2 C broccoli (about 8 oz), cut into small pieces

Extra virgin olive oil, 1 tbsp (0.5 oz).

1 chopped red onion, fine (about 2 oz).

2 tsp curry powder (0.2 oz)

1 tsp turmeric powder (0.1 oz)

1 tsp fresh grated ginger (0.1 oz)

1/2 C coconut milk (about 4 oz)

To taste, add salt and black pepper.

Citrus juice (optional, for garnish).

Preparation:

For instructions on how to prepare the quinoa, please refer to the package it came in. In most cases, it can be prepared by boiling it in two cups of water for fifteen to twenty minutes or until it has reached the desired doneness and the water has been absorbed.

During the time that the quinoa is being prepared, olive oil should be heated in a nonstick skillet over medium heat.

After adding the chopped onion, continue to cook for another two to three minutes or until the onion becomes transparent.

Stir in the curry powder, the turmeric, and the ginger. To allow the taste of the spices to develop, simmer for a further 2 minutes.

When the broccoli is ready, add it and cook for another 5-7 minutes.

Stir thoroughly after adding the coconut milk to the pan. Allow it to simmer for a further 2 to 3 minutes or until the sauce slightly thickens.

Add salt and black pepper to taste to the fish while it cooks.

Serve the curried salmon over the cooked quinoa and top the dish with the broccoli and coconut sauce. If desired, squeeze a little fresh lemon juice over the salmon before serving.

Nutritional Plan (per serving):

Cal: about 400 Cal.

Fat: 16g (about 36% of total Cal.)

PROT: 36g (about 34% of total Cal.)

Carbs: 31g (about 30% of total Cal.)

Fiber: 5g

Chicken Curry with Curried Vegetables and Brown Rice

Ingredients: Servings: 4

16 oz (4 breasts) of chicken breast, diced

1 C broccoli, cut into florets (roughly 4 ounces)

1 C carrots, thinly sliced (about 4 oz)

1 C cauliflower, cut into florets (about 4 oz)

1 onion, chopped (about 4 oz)

2 minced garlic cloves.

Coconut milk, 1 C (about 8 oz).

2 tbsp of red curry paste (about 1 oz)

2 tbsp of olive oil (about 1 oz)

2 C of cooked brown rice (about 8 oz)

To taste, add salt and black pepper.

Garnish with fresh cilantro (optional).

Preparation:

In a large skillet that does not stick, olive oil ought to be warmed up over medium-high heat. When it has reached a translucent state, add the onion and garlic and continue to sauté for another two to three minutes.

After the chicken has been cooked through and has developed a golden brown color, add the chicken cubes and continue to boil for another 5 to 7 minutes. It is necessary to remove the chicken from the pan and set it aside.

After the onion and garlic have been cooked for a few minutes, the red curry paste should be added to the same pan and cooked for an additional one to two minutes while being completely combined with the onion and garlic.

After adding the coconut milk to the pan that already contained the curry paste, give it a good stir. After briefly coming to a boil, reduce the heat to low and simmer for the next five minutes.

In the same pan in which the curry sauce is being prepared, cauliflower, carrots, and broccoli should be added. Cook with the lid on for ten to twelve minutes or until the veggies reach the desired crisp-tender consistency.

To warm up the chicken, put it in the skillet with the veggies that have already been cooked. Cook for an extra two to three minutes.

Serve brown rice that has been cooked with chicken curry and vegetables on top. If desired, add some fresh cilantro as a garnish.

Nutritional Plan (per serving):

Cal: about 450 Cal.

Fat: 16g (about 32% of total Cal.)

PROT: 32g (about 29% of total Cal.)

Carbs: 45g (about 39% of total Cal.)

Fiber: 7g

....

Quinoa Bowl with Smoked Salmon and Avocado

Ingredients: Servings: 4

1 C of raw quinoa (5 oz)

2 C of water

8 oz smoked salmon

2 ripe avocados, cut into slices

2 C fresh spinach (2 oz)

1 finely sliced cucumber.

Thinly sliced red onion, half.

One-fourth C of roasted sunflower seeds (1 oz).

Olive oil, 1/4 C (2 oz).

Two lemons juiced.

To taste, add salt and black pepper.

2 tbsp fresh chives, finely chopped

Preparation:

First, get the quinoa ready to eat. After giving it a thorough washing under running water, put it in a saucepan along with two cups of water. Bring to a boil, then immediately turn the heat down to low and cover the pot. The quinoa should be cooked for 15 to 20 minutes or until the water has been absorbed and the quinoa has reached the desired doneness. The quinoa should be fluffed with a fork, and then it should be placed aside to chill.

In a small bowl, whisk together the olive oil, lemon juice, salt, black pepper, and chives to make the lemon vinaigrette. Completely combine, then set aside.

Make thin strips of smoked salmon.

In a large bowl, combine cooked quinoa, smoked salmon, avocado slices, fresh spinach, cucumber slices, and red onion slices.

Pour the lemon vinaigrette over the ingredients in the bowl. Stir gently so that everything is well seasoned.

Divide the mixture among 4 individual bowls.

Sprinkle toasted sunflower seeds over each bowl.

Serve immediately and enjoy this quinoa bowl with smoked salmon and avocado.

Nutritional Plan (per serving):

Cal: about 490 Cal.

Fat: 29g (around 53% of the total Cal.)

PROT: 16g (around 15% of the total Cal.)

Carbs: 45g (around 32% of the total Cal.)

Fiber: 9g

Turkey Taco with Lemon Yogurt Sauce

Ingredients: Servings: 4

12 corn or whole wheat tortillas (about 6 oz)

1 lb ground turkey (16 oz)

Olive oil, 1 tablespoon.

One tiny red onion cut finely.

2 minced garlic cloves.

1 tsp of ground cumin.

Smoked paprika, 1 teaspoon.

A half-teaspoon of cayenne (or to taste).

To taste, add salt and black pepper.

1 C coarsely chopped red cabbage (4 oz).

1 C grated carrots (4 oz)

1 cucumber, thinly sliced

1 C plain Greek yogurt (8 oz)

One lemon juice.

2 tsp of finely chopped fresh mint leaves.

Hot sauce (optional)

Preparation:

In a large skillet that does not stick, olive oil ought to be warmed up over medium-high heat. After the onion has become translucent, add the minced onion and garlic and continue to boil for another two to three minutes.

When the ground turkey is thoroughly cooked and golden brown, add it to the skillet and heat it, breaking it up with a wooden spoon.

Ground turkey should be spiced with cumin powder, smoked paprika, cayenne, salt, and black pepper. For the flavors to meld, heat for a further two to three minutes after stirring thoroughly. Heat has been removed; set aside.

The yogurt sauce should be made in a sizable basin. Lemon juice, chopped mint leaves, Greek yogurt, and salt and pepper to taste should all be combined. Blend thoroughly until the sauce is smooth.

Lightly heat the tortillas in a hot skillet for about 20 to 30 seconds per side or until they are hot but not crispy.

Assemble the tacos: place a portion of spiced ground turkey on each tortilla, then add shredded cabbage, grated carrots, and a few slices of cucumber.

Pour a generous spoonful of lemon yogurt sauce over each taco. Add hot sauce if you want an extra touch of flavor.

Fold the tortillas in half and serve your turkey tacos with lemon yogurt sauce immediately.

Nutritional Plan (per serving):

Cal: about 330 Cal.

Fat: 9g (about 25% of total Cal.)

PROT: 20g (about 25% of total Cal.)

Carbs: 42g (about 50% of total Cal.)

Fiber: 5g

Grilled Tofu with Cabbage and Ginger Salad

Servings: 2
Ingredients

8 oz extra firm tofu, cut into cubes

6 oz cabbage, finely chopped

2 oz carrots, grated

2 oz red onion, thinly sliced

1 tbsp fresh grated ginger

Olive oil extra virgin, 2 tablespoons.

Apple cider vinegar, 2 teaspoons.

1 tbsp of low-sodium soy sauce or tamari.

To taste, add salt and pepper.

Garnish: toasted sesame seeds (optional).

Preparation:
Tofu should be cooked until golden brown all over on a hot, nonstick griddle or skillet.

Shredded cabbage, grated carrots, and thinly sliced red onion should all be combined in a big bowl.

To make the vinaigrette, combine the grated ginger, tamari, salt, and pepper in a small container, along with the olive oil, apple cider vinegar, and tamari.

Give the coleslaw a good toss after adding the vinaigrette.

Top the salad with the grilled tofu.

If desired, add toasted sesame seeds as a garnish.

As a light dinner, serve grilled tofu with coleslaw and ginger.

Nutritional Plan (per serving):

Cal: about 330 Cal.

Fat: 23g (about 63% of total Cal.)

PROT: 14g (about 17% of total Cal.)

Carbs: 21g (about 20% of total Cal.)

Fiber: 7g (about 28% of total Cal.)

··

Tomato and Basil Soup with Tofu Croutons

Servings: 2
Ingredients

8 oz ripe tomatoes, cut into pieces

2 oz onion, chopped

2 oz carrots, shredded

2 cloves of garlic, minced

4 oz. of cubed, extremely firm tofu.

veggie broth, 2 cups.

fresh basil leaves, 1/4 cup.

Olive oil extra virgin, 2 tablespoons.

To taste, add salt and pepper.

Whole wheat bread slices for the croutons.

Preparation:

In a saucepan set over moderate heat, olive oil should be warmed up.

Add the carrots, onion, and garlic that have been chopped. Cook veggies until they reach the desired degree of tenderness.

After adding the diced tomatoes, continue to cook the mixture for a few more minutes.

Once everything has been added to the pot, the vegetable broth should be brought to a boil. Maintain a low heat and let the mixture simmer for around 15 to 20 minutes.

It is recommended to use a frying pan to warm the tofu cubes, after which they should be cooked until golden brown on all sides.

Blend the soup with an immersion blender until it reaches the desired consistency. Combine with the leaves of basil.

To achieve your desired flavor, tweak the salt and pepper.

For croutons, toast some pieces of whole wheat bread.

Serve the tomato basil soup with tofu croutons.

Nutritional Plan (per serving):

Cal: about 280 Cal.

Fat: 14g (about 45% of total Cal.)

PROT: 12g (about 17% of total Cal.)

Carbs: 30g (about 38% of total Cal.)

Fiber: 6g (about 24% of total Cal.)

Chickpea and Roasted Vegetable Salad with Tahini Sauce

Servings: 2
Ingredients

6 oz cooked chickpeas (rinsed and drained)

4 oz zucchini, cut into strips

4 oz. of chopped mixed peppers.

2 oz of thinly sliced red onion.

2 oz of radicchio, thinly sliced.

Fresh spinach, 2 ounces.

Roasted pumpkin seeds in two tablespoons.

Toasted sesame seeds, 2 teaspoons.

Olive oil extra virgin, 2 tablespoons.

Tahini sauce, two teaspoons.

One lemon juice.

To taste, add salt and pepper.

Preparation:

Put the oven temperature to 400 degrees Fahrenheit (200 degrees Celsius).

Arrange the zucchini and bell pepper strips in a neat pattern on a baking sheet that has been covered with parchment paper. Add some salt, pepper, and olive oil, then sprinkle with the seasonings.

Bake the vegetables for 20 to 25 minutes or until they have become soft and have developed a light browning on some of their surfaces.

It is recommended that the cooked chickpeas, red onion, radicchio, spinach, and roasted vegetables be mixed together in a large bowl.

To make the vinaigrette, take a small bowl and mix together the tahini sauce, lemon juice, olive oil, and seasonings of your choice (salt and pepper).

Mix the salad thoroughly with the vinaigrette before serving.

With toasted sesame seeds and pumpkin seeds for garnish, plate the chickpea salad and roasted veggies.

Nutritional Plan (per serving):

Cal: about 350 Cal.

Fat: 20g (around 51% of the total Cal.)

PROT: 13g (around 15% of the total Cal.)

Carbs: 34g (around 34% of the total Cal.)

Fiber: 9g (about 36% of total Cal.)

··

Baked Salmon with Lemon and Capers Sauce

Servings: 2
Ingredients

2 salmon fillets (about 6 oz each)

2 tsp of washed and drained capers.

2 minced garlic cloves.

One lemon juice.

Extra virgin olive oil, 1 tablespoon.

1 tsp finely minced fresh parsley.

To taste, add salt and pepper.

Preparation:

Put the oven temperature to 400 degrees Fahrenheit (200 degrees Celsius).

Capers, minced garlic, lemon juice, extra virgin olive oil, chopped parsley, and a

pinch of salt and pepper should be mixed together in a bowl to make the sauce.

Arrange the salmon fillets in a single layer on a baking sheet that has been covered with baking paper.

Pour the lemon-caper sauce over the salmon before serving.

Cook the salmon in the oven for fifteen to twenty minutes or until it can be easily flaked apart.

As a light meal, serve baked fish with a lemon caper sauce.

Nutritional Plan (per serving):

Cal: about 300 Cal.

Fat: 15g (about 45% of total Cal.)

PROT: 35g (about 47% of total Cal.)

Carbs: 5g (about 8% of total Cal.)

Fiber: 1g (about 4% of total Cal.)

Lentil and Tomato Salad

Ingredients (for 2 servings):

4 oz of dried red lentils

8 oz ripe, diced tomatoes

Olive oil extra virgin, 2 tablespoons.

A single tsp of apple cider vinegar.

1 garlic clove, minced finely.

One tbsp of dried oregano.

To taste, add salt and freshly ground black pepper.

For garnish, use fresh basil leaves.

Preparation:

Rinse red lentils under running water and cook them according to the instructions on the package. Red lentils typically take 15 to 20 minutes to cook. Let them cool after draining them.

Red lentils that have been cooked and diced tomatoes are combined in a big bowl.

In order to make a vinaigrette, put the garlic, dried oregano, salt, and pepper in a small bowl along with the olive oil, apple cider vinegar, and apple cider vinegar.

To evenly spread the vinaigrette, drizzle it over the lentil and tomato salad and gently mix.

Garnish with fresh basil leaves.

Serve Lentil and Tomato Salad as a light and anti-inflammatory dish.

Nutritional Plan (per serving):

Cal: about 325 Cal.

Fat: 10g (about 28% of total Cal.)

PROT: 15g (about 18% of total Cal.)

Carbs: 45g (about 54% of total Cal.)

Fiber: 16g (about 64% of total Cal.)

Grilled Salmon with Spinach Salad and Strawberries

Ingredients: Servings: 4

4 salmon fillets (about 24 oz)

8 C of fresh spinach (about 8 oz)

2 C fresh strawberries, sliced (about 12 oz)

1/2 C pecans, toasted and chopped (about 2 oz)

1/4 C red onion, thinly sliced (about 1.5 oz)

1/4 C goat cheese, crumbled (about 1.5 oz)

2 tbsp balsamic vinegar (about 1 oz)

2 tbsp of extra virgin olive oil (about 1 oz)

Salt and black pepper to taste.

Preparation:

Adjust the temperature of the grill to medium-high, and then apply a thin layer of olive oil on the grates.

After being coated in olive oil, salmon fillets are given a seasoning of salt and black pepper before being cooked.

After being grilled for three to four minutes on each side, the flesh of the salmon should easily break apart when tested with a fork. After being cooked, the salmon should be removed from the grill and set aside.

In a sizable bowl, all of the following ingredients—raw spinach, sliced strawberries, toasted walnuts, sliced red onions, and goat cheese—should be mixed together.

Vinaigrette can be produced by blending balsamic vinegar and extra virgin olive oil in a small bowl. This creates the dressing for the vinaigrette. Dress your salad with this easy vinaigrette instead of store-bought dressing.

Serve the grilled salmon over the spinach and strawberry salad.

Nutritional Plan (per serving):

Cal: about 450 Cal.

Fat: 27g (about 54% of total Cal.)

PROT: 35g (about 31% of total Cal.)

Carbs: 18g (about 15% of total Cal.)

Fiber: 5g

These are just a few of the many anti-inflammatory recipe options you can experiment with. Experimenting with fresh, antioxidant-rich ingredients such as herbs, spices, and a variety of vegetables can lead to tasty, health-beneficial meals.

Conclusions

We have come to the conclusion of our journey through the world of anti-inflammatory cooking for beginners. During this journey, we explored in detail the basic principles of nutrition that promote wellness and health without prescribing or promising medical cures.

We began by understanding what inflammation is and how it affects our health. We explored the basics of anti-inflammatory cooking, learning to recognize foods that can help reduce inflammation and those to avoid.

On our culinary journey, we explored many delicious recipes designed especially for beginners. We started the day with nutritious breakfasts such as Coconut and Mango Smoothies and continued with light and tasty lunches such as Quinoa Salad with Chickpeas and Vegetables. We ended the day with tasty dinners like Baked Salmon with Lemon and Capers Sauce.

But, anti-inflammatory cooking is more than just a collection of recipes; it is a lifestyle that embraces the balance between nutrition, physical activity, and mental well-being. We discussed how to incorporate strategies such as meditation, deep breathing, regular physical activity, and relaxation practices into everyday life to promote overall well-being.

Each step of this journey is designed to help you make more informed food decisions and improve your health without promising miracle solutions. The key is balance, variety, and awareness.

I wish you a culinary future filled with delicious flavors and food choices that will help you keep a healthy body and inflammation under control. Before making any significant alterations to your diet or lifestyle, you should always make an appointment with your primary care physician.

28 Days Plan

Day	Breakfast	Lunch	Snack	Dinner
1	Oats with Berries and Flaxseed	Spinach Salad with Grilled Chicken and Almonds	A handful of almonds	Red Lentil and Tomato Soup
2	Oats with Fresh Fruit and Walnuts	Barley Salad with Tomatoes and Cucumbers	Baby carrots with hummus	Smoked Salmon Bowl with Avocado and Brown Rice
3	Avocado Toast with Egg and Dried Tomatoes	Curried Tofu Bowl with Hummus	A small piece of cheese	Quinoa Salad with Chickpeas and Roasted Vegetables
4	Couscous Bowl with Grilled Chicken and Vegetables	Baked Salmon with Lemon Quinoa and Spinach	Celery sticks with peanut butter	Grilled Salmon with Curry and Mango Sauce
5	Buckwheat Bowl with Roasted Vegetables	Chicken Curry Salad with Almonds	One serving of vanilla yogurt	Chickpea and Roasted Vegetable Salad with Tahini Sauce
6	Chicken Teriyaki Bowl with Vegetables	Curried Chickpea Salad	A handful of almonds	Quinoa Bowl with Sesame Tofu
7	Quinoa Bowl with Smoked Salmon and Avocado	Melon with Ham	Carrot sticks with hummus	Smoked Salmon Bowl with Avocado and Brown Rice

Day	Breakfast	Lunch	Snack	Dinner
8	Quinoa Bowl with Curried Tofu and Roasted Vegetables	Mini Frittatas with Tomato and Basil	A pear	Chickpea and Roasted Vegetable Salad with Tahini Sauce
9	Smoked Salmon Bowl with Avocado and Brown Rice	Buckwheat Salad with Roasted Vegetables and Hummus	A handful of walnuts	Pesto Quinoa Salad with Tomatoes and Black Beans
10	Bruschetta with Tomatoes and Basil	Spring Quinoa with Grilled Vegetables and Lemon Sauce	A small piece of cheese	Seaweed and Cucumber Salad
11	Bruschetta with Tomato and Mozzarella Cheese	Grilled Chicken Roll with Sweet Chili Sauce	Baby carrots with hummus	Beet Salad with Spinach and Walnuts
12	Beet Carpaccio with Walnuts and Goat's Cheese	Baked Salmon with Lemon and Capers Sauce	One serving of vanilla yogurt	Quinoa with Curried Vegetables
13	Crostini with Goat's Cheese and Honey	Quinoa with Turmeric Chicken and Roasted Vegetables	A handful of almonds	Quinoa and Beet Salad with Cumin Hummus
14	Tomato and Basil Crostini	Curried Tofu with Grilled Vegetables	Celery sticks with peanut butter	Grilled Chicken Roll with Sweet Chili Sauce
15	Omelette with Herbs and Tomatoes	Spinach Salad with Grilled Salmon and Almonds	A pear	Chickpea and Tomato Salad with Tuna

Day	Breakfast	Lunch	Snack	Dinner
16	Frittata with Spinach and Tomatoes	Spinach Salad with Grilled Salmon and Avocado	Carrot sticks with hummus	Quinoa Bowl with Smoked Salmon and Avocado
17	Vegetable Frittata with Avocado	Grilled Chicken Salad with Quinoa and Avocado	A handful of walnuts	Chickpea and Tomato Salad
18	Spinach and Banana Smoothie	Chicken Salad with Avocado and Quinoa	A small portion of dried fruit	Buckwheat Salad with Roasted Vegetables and Hummus
19	Guacamole with Whole Grain Corn Chips	Tomato and Cucumber Quinoa Salad with Lemon Yogurt Dressing	Baby carrots with hummus	Curried Tofu Bowl with Roasted Vegetables
20	Pea Guacamole with Corn Chips	Beet Salad with Spinach and Walnuts	A pear	Lentil and Tomato Salad
21	Beet Hummus with Vegetable Sticks	Curried Chickpea Salad with Grilled Chicken	Celery sticks with peanut butter	Salmon Tacos with Avocado Sauce
22	Chickpea Hummus with Vegetable Sticks	Curried Chickpea Salad	A handful of almonds	Quinoa Bowl with Curried Tofu and Roasted Vegetables
23				
	Seaweed and Cucumber	Barley Salad with Tomatoes	Baby carrots	Quinoa Salad with

Day	Breakfast	Lunch	Snack	Dinner
	Salad	and Cucumbers	with hummus	Chickpeas and Avocado
24	Beet Salad with Spinach and Walnuts	Chicken Curry Salad with Almonds	A small portion of dried fruit	Curried Tofu Bowl with Broccoli and Spinach
25	Curried Chickpea Salad	Curried Chickpea Salad with Grilled Chicken	A handful of walnuts	Quinoa Salad with Grilled Vegetables and Feta Cheese
26	Curried Chickpea Salad with Grilled Chicken	Melon with Ham	Carrot sticks with hummus	Smoked Salmon Bowl with Avocado and Brown Rice
27	Chickpea and Beet Salad with Cumin Hummus	Mini Frittatas with Tomato and Basil	A pear	Chickpea and Roasted Vegetable Salad with Tahini Sauce
28	Chickpea and Tomato Salad with Tuna	Spring Quinoa with Grilled Vegetables and Lemon Sauce	A handful of almonds	Quinoa Bowl with Sesame Tofu

Printed in Great Britain
by Amazon